TROTSKY IN EXILE

First performed in Germany in 1970, Peter Weiss's new play portrays a vast sweep of the history of the Russian Communist Party. The vantage point is that of Trotsky in retirement and isolation, just before his death in 1940. As the action moves backwards and forwards in time, episodes from various periods of his life are shown: his imprisonment under the Tsarist regime in 1902, the Revolution of 1905, exile with Lenin in Zurich, the October Revolution, his expulsion from Russia in 1928, and the final years of exile in France, Norway and Mexico. Trotsky's life emerges as one of personal struggle and personal tragedy, but it is the gigantic political struggle and the gigantic political tragedy that occupy the centre of the stage.

The photograph on the back of the cover is reproduced by courtesy of the German Embassy in London.

Peter Weiss

TROTSKY IN EXILE

Translated by
GEOFFREY SKELTON

METHUEN & CO LTD
11 NEW FETTER LANE LONDON EC4

2 085495 21

Originally published in German as 'Trotzki im Exil' in 1970
by Suhrkamp Verlag, Frankfurt am Main
© Suhrkamp Verlag, Frankfurt am Main 1970
This translation first published in Great Britain
by Methuen and Co Ltd in 1971
Translation Copyright © 1971 by Geoffrey Skelton
Printed in Great Britain
by Cox & Wyman Ltd, Fakenham, Norfolk

SBN 0416 16630 x (Hardback)
SBN 0416 16620 2 (Paperback)

Chronology of Trotsky's Life

1879   Lev Bronstein born 7.11 (old calendar 26.10) at Yanovska (Ukraine). His father was a Jewish farmer.

1897   At Odessa University founds the Southern Russian Workers' Union.

1898   Sent to prison in Kherson for political activities. Transferred to Odessa.

1899   Sentenced to Siberia for four years (Ust-Kut, then Verkholensk).

1900   Awaiting deportation, marries Alexandra Sokolovskaya. Daughter Zinaida born.

1902   Daughter Nina born. Escapes from Siberia with a false passport made out in the name of Trotsky. Visits Lenin in London.

1903   Meets Natalia Sedova in Paris. (Though known as his wife, she was never married to Trotsky.)

1905   Returns to Russia secretly with Natalia. Joins the first soviet in Petersburg. Arrested.

1906   His son Lev Sedov born. Sentenced to Siberia for life. Escapes from convoy and joins Lenin in Finland.

1907   Settles in Vienna. His second son, Sergey Sedov, born.

1914   At outbreak of war moves with family via Switzerland to France.

1916   Expelled from France and deported to Spain.

1917   Arrives in New York with Natalia and their sons. After February Revolution permitted to return to Russia. Arrives in Petrograd on 17 May (old calendar 4 May).

       Appointed foreign minister in first Soviet government.

1918   Appointed war minister. Founds the Red Army.

1921   Naval insurrection at Kronstadt put down by force on Trotsky's orders.

1924   Death of Lenin.

1925 Resigns as war minister, though remains member of the Central Committee.

1926 Forms opposition within the party with Kamenev and Zinoviev. Expelled from Central Committee.

1928 Deported to Alma Ata (Turkestan) on charge of counter-revolutionary activity. Daughter Nina dies.

1929 Banished from Soviet Russian territory. Settles at Prinkipo, an island in the Sea of Marmara.

1933 Daughter Zinaida commits suicide. Moves to France. Settles incognito in Barbizon.

1934 Expelled from Barbizon. Settles at Domesne near Grenoble.

1935 Moves to Norway and settles at Vexhall near Hönne-foss.

1936 Moscow trials. Trotsky and Lev Sedov found guilty in absence of preparing and directing terrorist acts in Soviet Russia. Interned by Norwegians, then expelled. Sergey Sedov arrested and sent to Vorkuta, where he is believed to have died.

1937 Arrives in Mexico with Natalia and settles at Coyoacan near Mexico City with Diego Rivera. Moscow trials continue.

1938 Dewey Commission (the 'counter-trial') issues verdict finding Trotsky and Lev Sedov not guilty of the crimes for which they were condemned at the Moscow trials. Lev Sedov dies in France in mysterious circumstances.

1939 Leaves Rivera's house and settles at Avenida Viena outside Coyoacan.

1940 23 May: abortive attack on Trotsky's house.
      20 August: Jacson's attempt on Trotsky's life.
      21 August: Trotsky dies.

TROTSKY IN EXILE

Cast

LEV DAVIDOVICH TROTSKY
ALEXANDRA, his first wife
ZINAIDA VOLKOV, her daughter
NATALIA, his second wife
LEV SEDOV ⎫
SERGEY SEDOV ⎬ her sons
VLADIMIR ILYICH LENIN
NADEZHDA KRUPSKAYA, his wife
INESSA ARMAND, his assistant
SERMUKS ⎫
POZNANSKY ⎬ Trotsky's secretaries in the Soviet Union

RAKOVSKY ⎫
MRACHKOVSKY ⎬ Trotsky's friends, members of the opposi-
SMIRNOV ⎭ tion at the time of his banishment in 1927

DZERZHINSKY ⎫
MAKHAISKY ⎬ Trotsky's fellow prisoners in his first exile
LUZIN ⎭ at the turn of the century

PLEKHANOV ⎫
AXELROD ⎬ Founders of the party, participants in
DEUTSCH ⎬ the secret Brussels meeting, 1903
VERA ZASULICH ⎭

ARKADI KREMER ⎫
AKIMOV ⎪
MARTYNOV ⎬ Participants in the Brussels meeting,
ROZANOV ⎪ 1903
MARTOV ⎭

PARVUS, Trotsky's colleague in planning the permanent
revolution
FATHER GAPON, workers' leader in the revolution of 1905
COUNT WITTE, tsarist minister
EMMY HENNINGS ⎫ Founders of the Dada move-
HUGO BALL ⎬ ment, Zurich, 1915/16

TRISTAN TZARA
MARCEL JANCO
RICHARD HUELSENBECK
ANNA BLUME
} Founders of the Dada movement, Zurich, 1915/16

RADEK
KAMENEV
SVERDLOV
ANTONOV
RYKOV
ZINOVIEV
PYATAKOV
BUKHARIN
STALIN
} Bolsheviks

KHINCHUK
ABRAMOVICH
KUCHIN
PETERSON
} Participants in the all-Russian congress, October 1917

SHLYAPNIKOV
ALEXANDRA KOLLONTAI
} Representatives of the workers' opposition

BLUMKIN, former Social Revolutionary, later a Bolshevik and supporter of Trotsky

A NORWEGIAN DOCTOR

PROSECUTOR at the Moscow trials

ZAFONOVA, witness at the Moscow trials

SALAZAR, chief of the Mexican secret police

ALFRED ROSMER
JOSEPH HANSEN
HAROLD ROBINS
SYLVIA AGELOF
} Trotsky's colleagues and assistants in Mexico

DIEGO RIVERA, Mexican painter

ANDRE BRETON, surrealist, visiting Mexico

FRANK JACSON

In addition:

Unnamed prisoners, court officials, students, workers, soldiers, sailors, etc.

Act One

The basic scene is a room that could be anywhere, with a writing-desk covered with papers and books, a camp bed, trunks and packing-cases and a few widely spaced chairs.

TROTSKY is seated at the writing-desk reading a manuscript, pen in hand. This picture is repeated at various points during the play. It corresponds to the final moments of the play.

Various stages of Trotsky's life are depicted against this unchanging scene: periods of exile, meetings and disputes with key figures in the revolution. The beginning is explained by the end, which shows Trotsky, in retirement and isolation, just before his death. The actors' entrances are swift and sudden.

1. THE BANISHMENT

> TROTSKY *looks up from his papers. Enter* NATALIA, LEV SEDOV, SERGEY SEDOV, ZINAIDA VOLKOV, SERMUKS, POZNANSKY, SMIRNOV, MRACHKOVSKY, RAKOVSKY.

RAKOVSKY. I was at the Kazan railway station. Huge crowds. Mostly young people. Demonstrations. Cries of 'Long live Trotsky!' A huge picture of you on the engine. Clashes with the soldiers. Some injured. Some arrests. I hear you're not to be taken there, but to the Yaroslav station. Bukharin's in charge.

TROTSKY. Are the doors locked, Rakovsky?

RAKOVSKY. And bolted. They're already outside.

> *The others are meanwhile busy packing the trunks and cases.* SERMUKS *goes to the table and sits down, ready to write.*

TROTSKY. The Political Bureau is trying to make the banishment look like a voluntary agreement. That's what the people have been told. Important to destroy this legend. To show the true facts. And in a way that can't be hushed up or mis-represented. We'll force the enemy to use violence.

ZINAIDA. They're in the hall. Coming up the stairs.

TROTSKY *stands up.*

TROTSKY. The date, Sermuks.

SERMUKS. Sixteenth of January, nineteen twenty-eight.

SERMUKS *finishes writing, gathers the papers on the desk together.*

TROTSKY. Diary, writing things in the briefcase. Where are the dictionaries, Poznansky? English, German, French, Spanish. Have you put in enough pencils? Pens, ink?

LEV SEDOV. Time to get dressed, Father.

TROTSKY. Always ready to move on. Orders disturbed, re-stored. Materials China, India. South America. Liberation movements in the colonies. Struggle of the blacks in the United States. Papers on the International. No reports here on the state of the Indian party. Send them to me, will you, Smirnov? And, Rakovsky, send on the newspapers as fast as you can.

RAKOVSKY. If they don't transport us too.

ZINAIDA *comes in with an overcoat and a fur cap.*

ZINAIDA. Your coat, Father.

TROTSKY. Put it on the chair, Zina.

ZINAIDA. Quickly, Father.

TROTSKY. I shan't walk a step.

TROTSKY *sits down on the camp bed. The last papers and books are cleared from the desk and packed.*

NATALIA. A long quiet period for work. No telephone, no visitors. You can start in the train. You know how well you work in the train.

TROTSKY. Seryosha, have you put in the maps?

SERGEY. In a folder. With the press cuttings.

TROTSKY. I'll study Asia on the journey. Geography, economy, history. Glazmann, what is the latest from China? Where's Glazmann?

MRACHKOVSKY. Down below. They've arrested him.

ZINAIDA. They've broken down the door. They're coming.

An officer and some soldiers with drawn bayonets come in.

OFFICER. I have orders to fetch you.

MRACHKOVSKY. Kishkin – you of all people. Our escort on the journeys to the front. Haven't they degraded Trotsky enough?

OFFICER. Nobody cares now who built the Red Army, Mrachkovsky. Get ready, Citizen Trotsky.

MRACHKOVSKY. Kishkin. A model disciplinarian. Trotsky's pupil. Got his job to do.

TROTSKY. I insist on taking Glazmann and my other assistants with me.

OFFICER. The composition of the travelling party is our business.

Meanwhile the soldiers are rounding up the others. SERGEY *attempts to escape. There is a scuffle, and he is struck down.*

NATALIA. Seryosha.

She is held back by the soldiers. SMIRNOV *and* RAKOVSKY *try to help* SERGEY. *They are overpowered and dragged off. The officer signals to a soldier to dress* TROTSKY. *The soldier throws* TROTSKY's *coat over his shoulders and pushes the cap on his head.* TROTSKY *refuses to stand up. The soldiers lift him up and carry him forward.*
From the sides appear neighbours and townsfolk.

LEV SEDOV. Look, neighbours. They're carrying Comrade Trotsky away.

The soldiers drive the group on with rifle butts.

Look, citizens, they're carrying Comrade Trotsky through the streets.

A few railway workers at back.

Workers, look. They're taking Comrade Trotsky to Siberia.

SERGEY. Don't get on the engine. Refuse to move it.

> SERGEY *is dragged off.* ZINAIDA *follows him. The group is rounded up in the middle of the stage. Soldiers and workers force back the onlookers. The group is now alone.*

NATALIA. Snow in Alma Ata. White, smooth, dry. In the spring poppies everywhere. The steppes red with poppies.

SERMUKS. Alma Ata. No running water. No light. No made up roads. Just dirt. And lice.

POZNANSKY. Malaria in the summer.

LEV SEDOV. And plague. Rabid dogs.

NATALIA. Fruit trees in the garden. It smells of ripe apples.

MRACHKOVSKY. Mountains on the Chinese border.

> *The group disperses. Working materials are unpacked. Writing things, books, papers arranged on the desk.* TROTSKY *puts out pens and pencils and sits down at the desk. All the others move to back and off. Only* MRACHKOVSKY *remains, sitting huddled up.*
> TROTSKY *remains a few moments in his position at the desk as at the beginning.*

2. THE PENAL COLONY OF VERKHOLENSK

MRACHKOVSKY, DZERZHINSKY, MAKHAISKY, LUZIN, ALEXANDRA SOKOLOVSKAYA *and other nameless prisoners come in.* ALEXANDRA *proceeds to make up a bed of blankets and furs.* TROTSKY *is at the desk.*

TROTSKY. My fellow prisoners. Sometimes Natasha. Sometimes Alexandra. Exile. Banished by my own people. Banished by the Tsar. Siberia. Nearly thirty years ago. A new century was beginning. (*He brushes a hand over an open book.*) Cockroaches are reading Marx. Cockroaches eating *Das Kapital*. Alexandra, how are the children?

ALEXANDRA. Zina is asleep. Ninushka still feverish.

DZERZHINSKY. The new century. Signs of the coming storm. Awful portents. Russia. What a huge factory of ideas. And what despotism. Court, nobility, landowners, officers, overseers, foremen, police. Patriarchs all. Absolute power in the family. Over children, grandchildren. We must break it. But where are the free men to come from?

FIRST PRISONER. Is that right what they say in the *Iskra*? Workers can't rebel on their own. Need leadership. So the intellectuals must plan it for them.

SECOND PRISONER. Revolution starts in the streets.

FIRST PRISONER. Our planners. Local heroes. Students. Go out to the suburbs. Collect a few workers. Try to tell us how to take over our own factories. And don't know one end of a machine from the other.

MRACHKOVSKY. Yet everything grinds to a halt the moment the students are arrested. Or even go off on holiday. Not a murmur from below.

FIRST PRISONER. A handful of knowalls. What good have they ever done us? Churning out a few socialist ideas of their own. They haven't got through to the masses.

TROTSKY. You're suspicious of the students. It's true, they come from the middle classes. Where else? They're the only ones with the means and the time to read and learn. The worker sweats out his eleven or twelve hours a day. At the end has no energy left for learning. But think what is really happening. For the first time students are not using their knowledge to get themselves a comfortable place among their own class. They're turning it against the society that raised them. A bourgeois revolution beginning. Students taking sides with the workers. That means they're prepared

to go on to the next stage, to the revolution of the proletariat. That's why we need political leadership, a party. To
push *this* revolution on, to secure power for the workers.

FIRST PRISONER. You're still intellectuals. How many workers read your poems, Dzerzhinsky? Do they read your
learned tracts, Bronstein?

DZERZHINSKY. What does it matter where revolutionaries
come from? In the struggle for a classless society they soon
learn to forget their families. And one day it will be the sons
and daughters of the workers who go to the universities.

ALEXANDRA. What have you got against intellectuals? Aren't
they shut up here too in Verkholensk? Isn't it work to print
and distribute illegal pamphlets? To agitate? To build an
organization?

MAKHAISKY. Organization is the beginning of the end.

TROTSKY. The strikes – they show the fight has really begun.
But economic struggle isn't political struggle. The individual
cells inside the factories must be brought together.

MAKHAISKY. And that puts an end to spontaneous movement.
Look at Germany: it's the party that's strong there. A bunch
of opportunists, starting with their Bernstein. No power for
the workers, but alliance with the middle class. Not revolution but liberalism.

LUZIN. All those theorizers sitting outside. Plekhanov, Axelrod, Martov, Lenin. Telling everybody revolution must
begin in the industrial states. *This* is where it will begin.
Here in medieval, Asiatic Russia.

TROTSKY. Spontaneity is not enough, Makhaisky. Spontaneity
is rebellion born of rage, despair, hunger. That is not what
we mean by revolution. Risings of that kind went out with
the Paris Commune. They help nobody but the bourgeoisie.
Not because *they* are revolutionaries, but because they're
what they are. They've got their hands on property, on
schools, the press, the army. We could mount the barricades, yes. But what we really need is a general strike, mass

meetings, demonstrations. And the army. Without the army on our side nothing will be achieved in our lifetime.

MAKHAISKY. With the old state creaking in every joint? Shoot a minister and the Tsar shivers with fright.

TROTSKY. Our concern is not killing ministers, but the total destruction of the monarchy.

MAKHAISKY. A party of the kind you want will be just a new form of tyranny. A chosen few – officials, technicians, scientists – fleecing the proletariat. Maybe you talk now of abolishing the state. But you'll forget all that when you have your own instrument of power. We must go on as we began – to smash the state, its institutions and its bureaucracy.

TROTSKY. Language of the past century, Makhaisky. Progress lies with the researchers, the mathematicians, the administrators.

LUZIN. Once people see what's good for them, the power problem is solved. We don't need a central committee to show them that.

MAKHAISKY. We must fight the state with the same weapons it uses against us. Terrorize the fat bosses, the greedy moneybags, the governmental gasbags. Terrorize the conformists. Then they'll show us what they're really like. Everyone will recognize their ugly mugs.

LUZIN. We don't need the army. Bombs are easy to make. A bit of nitric acid, a bit of potassium chlorate in a bottle, and the law courts, the barracks, the Bank of Russia go up in flames.

TROTSKY. Your explosives are no substitute for the masses, Luzin. Some of you will get burned, die your individual hero's deaths. But you won't win the workers to your side.

A soldier in fur cap and coat with collar turned up, a rifle in his hand, leads in another prisoner. LUZIN *goes to the soldier.*

LUZIN. Hey, you. How can you do things like this? What's your father? A peasant? A worker?

The soldier threatens him with the rifle. LUZIN *draws a knife.*

What, so you'd shoot your own brothers? How do the officers treat you? What pay do you get? You'd defend your own oppressors, would you – against us?

The soldier raises his rifle to shoot. Several of the prisoners throw themselves to the floor. TROTSKY *shelters behind the desk.* LUZIN *goes for the soldier with his knife. The soldier shoots, but* LUZIN *is not hit. They wrestle together. Other soldiers come in.* LUZIN *is beaten up and dragged off.*

ALEXANDRA. Luzin will be taken to the Katorga. If they don't kill him straight away. A schoolteacher. So much still he could have done for us.

All except DZERZHINSKY *and* MRACHKOVSKY *to back, where they sit or lie down on the floor.*

TROTSKY. Four whole years. Anyone might think we loved our prison. But we love it just as little as a drowning man loves the bottom of the sea. We shall not be silenced. History. This terrible machine. It grinds slowly, agonizingly. Drinks our blood. Yes, it creeps along. Unbearable. We must summon up our strength. Push. Move it on. Anything but wait.

He gets up quickly.

MRACHKOVSKY. Time now, Bronstein.

DZERZHINSKY. Your turn to escape. The peasants will see you through. Hide you in a haycart. We'll stuff your bed with blankets. Say you're ill. Give you a few days' start.

TROTSKY. The children.

MRACHKOVSKY. We'll look after them. Alexandra's not alone.

DZERZHINSKY. You'll contact the groups in Irkutsk, Samara, Kharkov, Kiev. Then on through Vienna, Zurich and Paris to London. Lenin is expecting you.

MRACHKOVSKY. You've got your papers. What name have you put in the passport?

TROTSKY. Trotsky. The name of my prison warder in Odessa.

DZERZHINSKY, MRACHKOVSKY go to the back. NATALIA *joins them. A group of soldiers in heavy coats and fur caps enters and rounds up the prisoners. Only* TROTSKY *remains at front.*

NATALIA. They've taken Sermuks. Didn't even give him time to put on his boots. The GPU is interrogating him in the cellar.

TROTSKY turns violently towards the back. There the prisoners are being silently led or carried off one after another.

Lyova is already outside. Sending telegrams. But it won't help. They've taken Poznansky too. He just had time to give me the mail. Rakovsky has been banished to Astrakhan. Smirnov in the Caucasus. Seryosha is still under arrest in Moscow. News from Alexandra. Nina is seriously ill. Zina is with them.

TROTSKY. Nina was ill that time too. When I left Alexandra and the children in Siberia.

He sits down again at the desk. NATALIA *is alone at the back.*

Was it right to put my work first? Before everything: family, friendship, love? To see myself just as part of a historical process?

He arranges the papers on the desk, then sits a few moments as at the beginning of the play. Then he rises and comes forward. NATALIA *goes off.*

3. LONDON

TROTSKY. London. Nineteen hundred and two. Ten Holford Place.

NADEZHDA KRUPSKAYA *appears.*

NADEZHDA. Hardly the time for visits.

TROTSKY. Yes, it's very early. But it took me three months to get here. I can't wait now.

NADEZHDA. Vladimir Ilyich, the Pen has arrived.

TROTSKY. Nadezhda Krupskaya, the cabman's outside. I had no money to pay him.

NADEZHDA KRUPSKAYA *goes off.* LENIN *comes in and goes quickly to the desk.* TROTSKY *goes to meet him. Both sit down, and the conversation begins at once.*

The question being asked all over Russia: what should the party do? Is it to think, decide and act for the proletariat? The workers say nobody can tell them how to run their factories. Once the owners are wiped out, they'll set up their own organization.

LENIN. Hm. They can form trade unions. Can force the management into improving their conditions. But the irreconcilable differences between their interests and the system as a whole – that they will have to be shown from outside.

TROTSKY. They'll tolerate no party that tries to run them. They're already strong enough to impose conditions on society. The middle classes are brutal, greedy. But cowards. The proletariat will swamp the bourgeois revolution.

LENIN. Hm. How old are you?

TROTSKY. Twenty-three.

LENIN. Lev Davidovich, you're trying to cut corners. You're impatient. For Russia a bourgeois revolution is the necessary first step. To break down feudalism. Put through land reforms. We need a democratic republic before the working class can mobilize, prepare for battle. It's still a minority. Must join hands with the semi-proletariat, the peasants.

TROTSKY. It's too late now for a bourgeois revolution in Russia. The proletariat is ready to go. We can't wait for the capitalist stage to be developed. Wouldn't anyway bring it up

to European standards. In backward countries democracy
can be achieved only through the workers.

LENIN. At this stage a revolutionary government in Russia
could only be a coalition of parties. Even then the socialists
would be a minority. Extremely dangerous, your illusions.

TROTSKY. We must go out for socialist revolution from the
very start. For the dictatorship of the proletariat. Without
letting up. Until our attacks flood out and infect the movement in other countries.

LENIN. Lev Davidovich. You are called the Pen because you
express your thoughts quickly and easily. We need you for
the *Iskra*. To put over from here the ideas which will lead in
time to revolution. But revolutionaries who cannot move
slowly and patiently are bad revolutionaries. Anyone can be
a revolutionary once revolution has broken out. Much more
difficult and more valuable to be a revolutionary when conditions for open battle don't yet exist. Further. Revolutionary tactics must be based on a strictly objective evaluation of
the strength of all social classes. Years of disciplined work
underground.

TROTSKY. We must keep moving on a broad front. Try out
our own strength.

LENIN. Amateurism. The reputation of our revolutionaries in
Russia is being lost through amateurishness. Sloppy and
shaky on theory. Narrow-minded. Hiding their own deficiencies under talk of the inherent strength of the masses.
Unable to work to an overall plan. Losing precious time in
argument. Each in love with his own ideas. Vulnerable to the
political police. Split wide open in every successive raid.
(*He rises, pressing a hand to his forehead.*) Give us an organization of professional revolutionaries, and we shall turn
Russia upside down.

TROTSKY *also rises.* LENIN *presses both hands to his
temples.*

TROTSKY. Are you ill, Vladimir Ilyich?

LENIN. Come. Let's get on.

From back and sides enter workers, pedestrians, a few British sailors. LENIN *makes a sweeping gesture towards the front.*

Look at this London. City of the monopolists. Parliament. The Tower. The British Museum. But it's no longer quite all theirs. We have built our nests in the bookshelves. Begun to undermine it.

At back a speaker on a soap-box. An audience gathers round him.

SPEAKER. Say after me, brothers and sisters. Lead us.

AUDIENCE. Lead us.

SPEAKER. Lead us, oh Lord.

AUDIENCE. Lead us, oh Lord.

SPEAKER. Out of the kingdom of capitalism.

AUDIENCE. Out of the kingdom of capitalism.

SPEAKER. Into the realm.

AUDIENCE. Into the realm.

SPEAKER. Into the realm of socialism.

AUDIENCE. Into the realm of socialism.

LENIN. And here the other London. Our London. Two separate nations.

The sailors smile at some female workers.

FIRST FEMALE WORKER. Sailors from the *Terrible.*

SECOND FEMALE WORKER. Watching the procession, were you?

FIRST SAILOR. In Trafalgar Square.

SECOND FEMALE WORKER. Did you get a good sight of the king? Was he still looking pale? What was the queen wearing?

FIRST WORKER. Couldn't see her dress for diamonds.

SECOND FEMALE WORKER. He thanked God in St Paul's for his recovery. After long illness. I have been restored to life.

Laughter.

FIRST WORKER. Where've you come from? Where've you been keeping order now? South Africa? Aden? India? China?

PEDESTRIAN. Where'd the empire be without the British Navy?

SECOND SAILOR. Venezuela. Blockading the rebels.

FIRST SAILOR. The revolt's over now.

SECOND SAILOR. But another one coming up in Colombia.

FIRST SAILOR. The Yanks'll look after that.

SECOND WORKER. And Somaliland? That's our territory. They say there's a big fight going on. What's it called? National liberation movement.

FIRST WORKER. Clemenceau says the strikes in France could bring on a revolution. If only we had more unity, if only the workers were better organized. In a scientific way.

SECOND WORKER. A hundred thousand miners marched through the streets.

FIRST WORKER. And the police fired on them. A lot killed. The strike in Dunkirk is already over. They didn't even ask for their arrested comrades to be released. Seven hundred and eleven for going back to work and four hundred and eighty-one against.

LENIN. All the same, four hundred and eighty-one against.

FIRST FEMALE WORKER. In America the strike's now in its hundredth day. Listen what the president said – Roosevelt. (*She opens a newspaper.*) Think of the coming winter, he says. The coal stocks are already low. The strike is becoming the biggest danger our country has ever had to face. The burning question is, shall the fundamental and inextinguishable rights of people to be free be trodden underfoot by the brutal mob? People, that's the coalowners. Mob, that's us.

SECOND WORKER. Mitchell, the miners' leader, says the strike's to go on – right through the winter if necessary.

FIRST WORKER. But he's already sold out to the bosses. The mines are occupied by troops, not workers. Maybe he'll get a few more cents on their wages. But the unions, they're no more use than ours. (*He turns to* LENIN *and* TROTSKY.) Here are two comrades from Russia. (*Indicating* TROTSKY.) His wife and kids are still there.

THIRD WORKER. If my wife was in prison, I wouldn't know what to do.

LENIN. Do you tell them in the factory that you're a socialist?

FIRST WORKER. What do you think? If the boss found out, I'd be out of a job. I keep my mouth shut. Got the family to think of.

LENIN. And the changes?

FIRST WORKER. They'll come, by peaceful means. Socialism's on its way. No doubt of that. We don't need a revolution.

They disperse slowly. LENIN *and* TROTSKY *come forward.*

LENIN. Look, Lev Davidovich. Down there the city. Plenty of fog. Plenty of smoke. Here on Primrose Hill Marx used to go walking. Worked for the world. Lies buried down there. His manifesto. Now almost forgotten. They dig it out on public holidays, the workers' leaders in Europe. It sounds empty in their mouths.

> LENIN *presses his hands to his temples. He goes to the camp bed and lies down.* TROTSKY *leans against the desk. They are now alone.*

4. BRUSSELS

TROTSKY. Then came our differences. They lasted more than ten years. Terrible, insuperable differences. What were we after? In that granary in Brussels? July, nineteen-three. At that secret meeting among the fleas and rats.

LENIN. And police spies.

TROTSKY. Sitting on planks, sacks. Worn out. Sweating. Half out of our minds. Perhaps our quarrels were due just to nerves. The strain of living in exile.

LENIN. We had to form an all-Russian party.

TROTSKY. I didn't see then that strict centralism was necessary. The way you choked off the old campaigners. Axelrod, Zasulich, Martov. I hated you for that.

LENIN. Revolutionary centralism demands harsh measures. Can be hard on old comrades, individuals or groups. But the end result excuses all ruthlessness.

Enter the participants at the Brussels conference: PLEK-HANOV, AXELROD, DEUTSCH, MARTOV, VERA ZASULICH, ARKADI KREMER, AKIMOV, MARTYNOV, ROZANOV, PARVUS *and others. They sit down at the desk, on packing-cases, chairs, on the floor. During the discussion there is constant unrest: some scratch themselves, stand up, wave their arms, kick their legs, throw books in corners. Now and again a participant wanders about like a sleep-walker.* LENIN *sits down at the centre of the desk, between* PLEKHANOV *and* DEUTSCH.

Further. We must finish for good and all with these separate groups, and form a united party. Move on from niggling to real revolutionary work. Get rid of all the cliques, the internal sympathies and antipathies. Get rid of national separatism. We must form a single party capable of leading millions.

PLEKHANOV. The Jewish Federation insists on keeping its autonomy. If we allow that, then all other national minorities will demand similar independence, once our party has achieved victory. Central organization would go. Be replaced by federation.

TROTSKY. What has held the Jews together till now? Their religion. That is on the point of vanishing. Their special way of life, their customs. But these are the result of the conditions under which they have lived for centuries. A self-contained Jewish culture is out of place.

Protests.

And out of place too is their semi-fictional nationalism, with its culmination in Zionism.

KREMER. In the pogroms in Kishinev they've just killed and deported thousands more of us. We must have the right to protect ourselves.

TROTSKY. A self-contained Jewish community: that's ghetto thinking.

KREMER. You're a Jew yourself, Lev Davidovich.

TROTSKY. I am a socialist. If I was born a Jew, I still don't recognize a Jewish nationality. And I believe just as little in the racial peculiarities of the Jews. To solve the Jewish problem, you don't need to form a Jewish state, but to transform society radically throughout the world.

KREMER. We insist on electing our own central committee. We must decide for ourselves on all questions concerning our people. Have our own schools and meeting places.

TROTSKY. But not set up barriers, Arkadi Kremer. Break down barriers between races, religions, nationalities.

PLEKHANOV. Proletarian dictatorship. That means sweeping aside all groups and institutions standing in the way of the workers' interests.

KREMER. We haven't yet debated the question of dictatorship. The *Iskra* is trying to work out revolutionary strategy in advance.

PLEKHANOV. Dictatorship by the proletariat is a pre-condition of the social revolution. The proletariat must have complete political power in order to suppress all resistance.

AKIMOV. Over the parliamentary system as well?

PLEKHANOV. If, after the collapse of the monarchy, a constituent assembly is elected which is opposed to the revolutionary workers' government, then it must be set aside.

AKIMOV. Comrade Plekhanov, how do you reconcile dictatorship with the idea of a democratic republic, as laid down in the programme? What of the freedom of the press, of political parties, the rights of assembly? What of the principle of equality for all citizens? No other socialist party in Europe speaks of dictatorship.

PLEKHANOV. Because they're all reformist parties, Akimov. Against revolution.

MARTYNOV. So we, the representatives of all those now groaning under tsarist dictatorship, must ourselves assume the right to dictate?

LENIN. The revolutionary proletariat is entitled to restrict the political rights of the bourgeoisie to the same extent that the bourgeoisie now restricts the proletariat.

ROZANOV. Isn't democracy something absolute? A principle for which we are fighting unconditionally? Will the Russian workers' party suspend free elections?

PLEKHANOV. If temporary restrictions of democratic rights are necessary to protect the interests of the revolution, it would be a crime to hesitate.

Applause and protests.

LENIN. All declarations concerning equal rights are nonsense. We ourselves have been denied our rights long enough. Let's get on. The question of membership.

MARTOV. Lenin and Plekhanov are demanding a selective party. Identified with the illegal organization. Only people working actively in a branch of the organization will be admitted. A party of conspirators. Not a party of the working classes.

Signs of unrest.

LENIN. The party is the supreme organization within the

proletariat. It stands above all other organizations in the workers' movement. It is the spearhead of the masses. It must be formed on the basis of centralism.

TROTSKY. An authoritarian party to create an authoritarian state.

DEUTSCH. Listen to our Benjamin, otherwise known as Lenin's axe.

MARTOV. We demand a widely based party. Not a party of the élite. A party that accepts everyone who supports our programme.

Unrest, catcalls.

TROTSKY. The rule of the proletariat can only be achieved when all the workers are united inside the party. Then it will be the rule of an overwhelming majority, not the dictatorship of a chosen few. We shall go back to Russia and work to strengthen this party.

DEUTSCH. Moderate your optimism, Lev Davidovich. Stay outside Russia. Finish your education. Learn something of the world. Develop your gifts.

Laughter.

TROTSKY. When things start in Petersburg, Deutsch, I shall be there.

LENIN. The workers are also disorganized. By opening its doors too wide, the party will let in all the elements of weakness and indecision as well. The party needs only the most convinced and the most courageous. Martov's party would include all the people who haven't yet learnt their jobs. The class instinct of the masses. Yes. They will fight. But they can only win if they're led.

AKIMOV. You talk of the party and the proletariat as if they're two separate things. Party, one single dynamic collective body. Proletariat, an inert mass on which the party works.

Party is subject, proletariat is object. Is that the dictatorship of the working classes?

Laughter.

TROTSKY. When Lenin says dictatorship of the proletariat, he means dictatorship over the proletariat.

Uproar.

AXELROD. Lenin is trying to isolate the party.

ZASULICH. A Robespierre, leading the party to the Thermidor.

LENIN. Zasulich, Axelrod, Martov, enough of this petty bourgeois bickering. Anyone who tries to split the party will be thrown out. Our present need is for an underground organization that can stand up to the political police. A party of revolutionaries. Not of phrasemongers.

Applause. Catcalls.

TROTSKY. So the organization of the party becomes more important than the party itself. Instead of an organization, a central committee. In the place of a central committee, a dictator. The first head to fall under the guillotine will be the lion's head of Karl Marx.

Uproar.

PLEKHANOV. We will take a vote on the status of the party. We also recommend Lenin's proposal that the *Iskra* should be placed over the central committee.

PARVUS. The party journal should be under the central committee.

LENIN. Impossible, Parvus. They can't control us from Russia. Here we have a stable centre. We shall lead the fight from here.

PARVUS. Unrestricted rule by the party journal.

LENIN. Under present circumstances it can't be otherwise.

The vote is taken amid uproar. All except LENIN *and* TROTSKY *go to back and off.*

TROTSKY. A majority of two. Two votes separate the majority party from the minority party. A clear split. Bolsheviks and Mensheviks.

LENIN. We lead by right. In every democratic body the majority has the power of decision, however small its advantage.

TROTSKY. How could you allow the party to split?

LENIN. Not a split. A clear definition. On the one side the people who can't forget their bourgeois origins. Their liberalism. Their egoism. Pushing themselves forward with private arguments. Stuck firm in the past. On our side the people of the future. Caring nothing for individual gain or glory. The select. The practicians. In a tight revolutionary organization.

TROTSKY. And the party's founders flung out.

LENIN. An illegal movement bent on overthrowing the Tsar can't afford to hand out sinecures. To improve our efficiency we must drop the old guard. That you must understand. But you put too much trust in yourself. You'll come to grief one day if you don't learn to keep your opinions to yourself and accept the party decision.

> LENIN *lies down on the camp bed and puts an arm across his face. Four soldiers come in, wearing Red Army uniform, rifles on their backs. They march to the camp bed, lift* LENIN *up and carry him to back and off.*

5. NINETEEN HUNDRED AND FIVE

> *As the soldiers go off, a crowd streams in from the back. They carry icons, church flags. At their head* FATHER GAPON, *a bearded priest with a crucifix at his breast. They come forward slowly.*

FATHER GAPON. We, workers in the town of St Petersburg, come to you, our ruler, to seek justice and protection. We are wretched, cast down and overburdened with heavy work. For us the moment has come in which death is better than the continuance of suffering. We have laid down our work and told the factory owner that we will not work again until such time as our demands are fulfilled. We have come to the walls of your palace to plead with you: let the people rule this land in company with you. Command that representatives of all classes and estates in Russia come together to form a constituent assembly. If you will not grant our prayer, we intend, here before your palace, to die. Today, on the ninth of January, nineteen hundred and five.

Shots. Flight. The crowd reassembles, this time without FATHER GAPON. TROTSKY *climbs on the desk and turns to the crowd.*

TROTSKY. Workers, peasants. You heard what the Tsar had to say to you. Through the streets of Petrograd you came to him. Wearing your Sunday clothes. With your wives, children, parents. Two hundred thousand strong. You went down on your knees to him. But you did not pray there. There the Tsar answered you.

VOICES. Murderer. Storm the palace. Kill him. Him and his family.

TROTSKY. Peasants, remember what he has always said. In my country I am the first nobleman, the first landowner.

VOICES. And handed us over to his servants. He treats his dogs better.

TROTSKY. Workers. You have gone on strike in the printing works, the steel works, the textile factories. Now bring the whole country to a standstill. Turn general strike into an armed rebellion.

A troop of soldiers in tsarist uniform comes in.

Peasants. We must get the army on our side. Tell the soldiers, your sons, who live on the people's money, that they must not raise their rifles against us.

Shots. Some workers gather round TROTSKY *to protect him.*

Workers, peasants. Let us light throughout Russia the fire that no power on earth can put out. The fire of revolution.

Shots. TROTSKY, *surrounded by the group of workers, descends from the desk and moves to the side.*

Workers, peasants. You have forced the absolute ruler to promise you freedom. You have found a weapon against him – mass strikes. When you showed him who is really in charge of the factories he began to take fright. But there's no real freedom when officers still hold the keys to the arsenals. Force them to hand the keys over to their rightful owners.

VOICES. To the Putilov works. There's machine-guns there. To the powder factory.

A few soldiers in tattered uniforms come forward.

Mutiny in the Black Sea fleet. The red flag flying on the *Potemkin*.

FIRST SOLDIER. What did we do in Japan, in China? Seized the railways – for them there, the swine. Kept the ports open – for them. Thousands of us died. In Port Arthur. In Manchuria.

SECOND SOLDIER. The officers. Keep your mouth shut, they shout. Stay where you are. Shoot us down for protesting. We had to walk home. They swindled us out of our rations. The Red Cross steals our coats and boots.

TROTSKY. Where are your rifles?

SECOND SOLDIER. We threw them away.

TROTSKY. You should have kept them. We need rifles. The Tsar has lost his war. Now our war begins. The Tsar has lost his Chinese railway. His Port Arthur. Good. The weaker he becomes, the stronger are we.

VOICES. To the barracks. Long live the workers' and soldiers' councils.

A red flag at back. At the same time a troop of the Black Hundreds comes in.

The Black Hundreds. Watch out, they'll shoot.

One of the soldiers of the Black Hundreds jumps on a packing-case.

SOLDIER OF THE BLACK HUNDREDS. The welfare of our fatherland lies in absolute Russian sovereignty. The welfare of our fatherland lies in the preservation of the Orthodox Church. The welfare of our fatherland lies in the common sense of the people. Absolute Russian sovereignty stems from the common sense of the people. It is blessed by the church and justified by history.

Disturbance and catcalls during the speech. The soldiers of the Black Hundreds push the crowd together with raised rifles. TROTSKY is borne by workers to a raised place, where they cluster around him again.

TROTSKY. This is the freedom the sovereign promised. He promises a constitution and at the same time sends word to the Black Hundreds: don't spare the bullets. He promises us freedom of speech, but censorship continues. He promises education for all, but the universities are occupied by soldiers. The rights of the individual are assured, but the prisons are filled to overflowing.

VOICES. Amnesty. Amnesty. To the prisons.

Violent movement in the crowd. The soldiers advance threateningly. A worker, SHLYAPNIKOV, springs on the desk.

SHLYAPNIKOV. If the government wants to make peace with us, they must free the prisoners.

VOICES. If they let out a hundred today, they'll shut up a thousand tomorrow. Take the prisons by force.

COUNT WITTE *emerges from the crowd to mount a packing-case at back.*

WITTE. Brother workers, do not drag your country into disaster. Have pity on your wives and children. Pay heed to a man who means well by you.

SHLYAPNIKOV. Who is he to be so familiar? Calling the workers his brothers. Count Witte's no relation of ours.

Laughter.

WITTE. Return to the factories. The Tsar has issued a manifesto promising a new constitution.

SHLYAPNIKOV. Yes, now. When we've got him down.

TROTSKY. A manifesto from that hangman. We'll show you what we think of rubbish like that.

TROTSKY *tears up a sheet of paper. Shots. The crowd is scattered by the soldiers. Among those taken prisoner are* DEUTSCH *and* PARVUS. SHLYAPNIKOV *and* TROTSKY *are also held and pushed towards the desk. The crowd goes off.*
Judges and court officials come forward. The judges sit down at the desk. The prisoners are guarded by soldiers with fixed bayonets. A handbell is rung.

Yes, my lord judges. Our acts were revolutionary. We were encouraging a rebellion. But a mass rebellion can't be engineered, can't be staged. It creates itself. All we could do was give the people reasons for rebellion. Tell them open conflict was unavoidable. That we had been deceived all along the line. That we must snatch freedom for ourselves.

The soviets armed the workers for a direct attack on this instrument for mass murder you still call a government.

Indignation. The president rings his bell.

If the acts of violence practised by the army and the police, the mowing down of workers and peasants, if all this represents the governmental system of the Russian Empire, yes, then we admit to taking arms against this government. The laws, the courts of justice are still administered by this regime. And you, my lord judges, uphold them against us, the elected representatives of the working people. One day you will be called to answer for your conduct before our courts of justice, our people's tribunals.

Renewed bell-ringing. The judges go off. The prisoners are rounded up behind the desk. The soldiers retire. The prisoners slowly disperse. At back MRACHKOVSKY *and* NATALIA *are led on.* TROTSKY *sits down at the desk.*

6. SECOND BANISHMENT

The other prisoners sit down at back. Only NATALIA *comes slowly forward.* TROTSKY *orders the papers and books on the desk and carefully arranges the writing materials. He sits for a few moments in the position as at the beginning of the play.*

TROTSKY. Sometimes I find myself thinking the revolution is only hindering me from working systematically. As if the battle of ideas were more important to me than revolutionary activity. The writing, the printed impression of my thoughts more real than the actions outside. (NATALIA *comes up behind him.*) The cities, Natasha. The lights in the streets. The noise of trams. And, most of all, the smell of printers' ink. A freshly printed newspaper. The cities. Moscow. London. Zurich. Paris. Third period of exile. But before. Before we could still escape. Then we had the coming revolution to hope for. (NATALIA *puts a hand on his shoulder.*) Paris. When was it? Nineteen hundred and three. We were walking home.

NATALIA. Rue Gassendi, number forty-six.

TROTSKY. Crossing the Seine bridge. Two children had climbed over the railing. On the concrete plinth. And you, suddenly you climbed up the steep column. Very fast, not looking round, your skirt pulled up, without any effort, any awkwardness. I can see it now, in your high-heeled shoes. The children were amazed.

NATALIA. It was springtime. The sun was shining.

TROTSKY. Can we say before history that we led the revolution? No. It took us by surprise. Nineteen hundred and five. In Petrograd. Lenin arrived when the rising was an accomplished fact. Plekhanov didn't even trouble to come to Russia. Advised against taking arms. And the party? More than ever remote from the people, since the split. We didn't prepare the strike. It was decided in the factories. Election of workers' soviets. The first revolutionary factor.

NATALIA. You were there. They elected you their chairman. You were everywhere. With advice, speeches.

TROTSKY. We were their mouthpiece. The force behind was theirs. We talked. Thought we could express things better. Self-importance.

The other prisoners come slowly forward.

Gapon was the man. Son of a peasant, a Cossack. He led the workers to the Winter Palace. It wasn't to be a peasants' revolt. He knew it was the workers in the towns who would start the fight.

PARVUS. You know where they picked him up again, your Father Gapon? In Monte Carlo. Throwing his money around, your workers' leader. And where had he got it? From Count Witte. Let himself be bought for thirty thousand roubles, to spy for the police. He'd lost faith in the revolution. So he betrayed the revolutionaries instead.

DEUTSCH. He didn't succeed. I heard what became of him. Comrades enticed him to a villa on the Finnish border. And there they strung him up. Yes, he was hanging there over a month, his face to the wall.

TROTSKY. But still he started the revolution.

DEUTSCH. That was no revolution. Lev Davidovich, you stripling. Would we be sitting here, in Siberia, if that had been a revolution? We brought the bourgeoisie to power. Ourselves we let be caught. With us old people it's different. We can't run so fast. But you.

TROTSKY. You were among the founders of the party, Leo. Good that one at least is here. The others. Zasulich still dreaming of an alliance with the liberals. Martov lurching from side to side in his eternal doubts. Plekhanov flat on his face agitating now against Lenin as well as against me. But historians can record that in nineteen five Leo Deutsch, the old rebel, was there.

PARVUS. And, for the workers, back to the treadmill. When I have my hour of meditation, evenings, I see those neglected streets, those mouldy walls. And right next to them huge piles of riches. You hear them say: more, more, I want still more. They climb over each other. Ladies beat each other with umbrellas. Gentlemen hurl their top-hats in each other's teeth. And to all those creatures down in the gutters they say: Bravo, you workers, you did your job well. But now, if you don't mind, get out of the way. It's our turn now.

TROTSKY. You've no idea how they really live, Parvus. Even here in our prison we're better off than they. We're left alone. Allowed books to read. Free board and lodging. Miles away from all the rags and tatters. We are always out on an advanced front.

NATALIA. But you were among them. Thousands listened to your words. Carried you on their shoulders.

TROTSKY. Only now and again. We give expression to the
violence we come on. Then hardly remember what we said.
Are deaf.

DEUTSCH. Still, we got the eight-hour day established almost
everywhere.

TROTSKY. The workers didn't need us for that. After eight
hours they simply told their employers: We shall down tools
and leave. Up to then they had no rights. Now they laid
down the conditions.

PARVUS. The employers are finding counter-measures. Threats
of dismissal. Rise in wages followed by a rise in the cost of
food. Some of the workers are ready to negotiate. A ten-
hour day there, nine hours somewhere else.

SHLYAPNIKOV. The metal workers won't give in.

DEUTSCH. Mass strikes are just a momentary skirmish in a
lengthy campaign. Time for the rising has not yet come.
Not enough experience. The middle classes are joining
hands with international capital. Tsar and Kaiser rediscover-
ing their mutual interests. The working class unarmed.
What drove them to it? The feeling that they couldn't bear
existing conditions any longer. No real plan. Without the
party the energy of the masses disperses like steam.

TROTSKY. But power can be got from steam.

PARVUS. What happened in Petrograd will affect the whole of
Europe. This mouldering country is still part of the world
market. Now it's up to the workers' parties in the west.
Our proletariat needs a rest. But will hold on to what it's got.

TROTSKY. During the next wave workers' councils will be
formed all over the country. An all-Russian workers' soviet
will assume the leadership. History doesn't repeat itself. From
these fifty days a programme of action for the future will
be evolved. The army, the peasants brought into the revolution. The police, the bureaucrats dismissed. The people
armed. The soviets turned into organs of revolutionary
movement.

DEUTSCH. Siberian pipe-dreams. You Benjamin. Do you really believe that Russia is ripe for a socialist revolution?

TROTSKY. The Russian proletariat has shown itself to be the leading revolutionary force. It will set up its dictatorship, perhaps even before the western countries start to move.

MRACHKOVSKY. But what if the west leaves us high and dry? The Bolsheviks are reckoning on a long period of bourgeois democracy. The Tsar's throne is still only a little dented. The west will do all it can to support it. What will the answer be to that famous spark you think will set fire to Europe? More battleships. More guns. More troops to strategic points.

> PARVUS *has meanwhile been doing gymnastic exercises, stretching his arms, bending his knees, taking short steps backwards and forwards. Now he comes forward, laughing.*

PARVUS. Oh yes, the Bolsheviks. Already making contemptuous remarks about Trotskyism. A few even talking of the Jewish grapevine. Who else but us believes in the idea of permanent revolution? The facts are against us. There's that German social democrat, that whining Philistine Kausky. What weapons will he give the Russian workers? All right, there's Rosa Luxembourg too, but she's pretty much alone. Lev, things are looking bad. Though we are right. In the long run.

TROTSKY. The revolution is here to stay. The whole world shows its marks. A national revolution can't be isolated. It's a link in an international chain. Our defeat in Manchuria shows how strong Asia is. China will begin to push. India. The South American countries. Fighting will break out in the colonies. Of course there will be setbacks. The bloated capitalists are not yet demoralized. But they're beginning to get panicky. They'll start fighting each other, to protect their ill-gotten gains. They'll tear each other to pieces.

SHLYAPNIKOV. And us too. Who does the fighting for them? We do. Always we.

PARVUS has resumed his marching with short steps and swinging arms. Now he stands still.

PARVUS. Will we ever live to see it? The way from the madhouse to the peaceful realm of labour? I doubt it. The class problem: for the past fifty years the bourgeoisie has been busy turning it into a science. The worker's condition has been studied in the smallest detail, categorized, catalogued. Fat books full of case histories, rows of them in the state libraries. Misery worked out on paper as a mathematical exercise. That way you can discuss it without getting excited. When will the air supply run out? When will there no longer be enough food to sustain life? How many men, women and children can you put in one house without damaging their morals? At what point does tiredness begin to affect a worker's usefulness? So gradually the bottom limit of endurance is raised. And so it can go on for another fifty years. The worker feels happier and happier. Yet in the end has probably not got more out of it than the eight-hour day.

DEUTSCH. Get on with your exercises, Parvus. Harden your muscles. Steel yourself for escape. We haven't time to sit here on our haunches, spending months and years in talk and more talk.

PARVUS. Exactly, my dear escapological expert. I, like you, distrust ourselves. I may once have been disloyal to my own class, but socialism for me is still nothing more than an abstract principle. We talk about the masses. What do the masses really mean to us? Are they anything more than an anonymous heap of numbers? A sort of historic dust? What do I start to think of when I'm sick of the smell of poverty? Lugano. The chestnut woods. A house of my own there. Or Cannes, Nice. Coffee on the terrace. We're no better than Father Gapon. The sea. Can you imagine the sea? Deep blue. Smooth, gentle waves. Time now for my meditation. I'm off to the beach.

He goes to the back, walks up and down, stoops, mimes the throwing of a stone. DEUTSCH, SHLYAPNIKOV *and* MRACHKOVSKY *also go to the back. All go off except* NATALIA. TROTSKY *arranges the papers on his desk.* LEV SEDOV *comes in from the back.*

TROTSKY. The pencils. Why haven't the pencils been sharpened? Where is the red pencil, Lev? Why haven't the final pages been copied yet? Natasha, have you got my medicine?

NATALIA gives him a bottle of medicine and a glass of water. He pours a few drops into the glass, drinks and shudders. He feels his pulse.

Malaria. I shall die here of malaria.

LEV SEDOV hands him some letters and newspapers.

LEV SEDOV. We've had news from Alexandra, Father. Nina's worse. Zina is ill too. They've arrested her husband. Almost eight thousand of our people have been deported.

TROTSKY glances at the letters.

TROTSKY. Our situation. On one side a tyrannical bureaucracy. On the other an apathetic working class. Our closest friends, those who worked for the revolution, who played a decisive part in the creation of the Soviet Republic – all of them now inside its prisons or in exile. Some will give in. Yield to pressure. The others. Will they stand firm?

NATALIA. Nothing from Seryosha?

LEV SEDOV. Nothing.

TROTSKY reads a letter.

TROTSKY. Rakovsky writes about Dante. Yes, of course, the product of a fixed social environment. Of course. *Commedia,* prompted by specific class interests. But if it were simply a portrait of the ruling class in Florence in the thirteenth century, we could easily dismiss it. Historical document. But since a commentary on his own time, account of a psychological development, connects with our ideas. Transcends the time barrier. Yes. Was condemned to be burnt at the stake. Wrote in exile. Never allowed back.

An OFFICER *comes in.*

OFFICER. How are you, Lev Davidovich, Natalia Sedova? And you, Lyova? Looking well enough. But rather lonely here.

TROTSKY. As lonely as one cares to make it.

TROTSKY *stands up, but does not approach the* OFFICER.

OFFICER. Don't you think that something could be done? Some gesture of reconciliation?

TROTSKY. Reconciliation? There can be no talk of reconciliation. Not because I don't want it. But because it's not within the possibilities of the opponent. I will tread the path on which bureaucracy has set me right to the end.

OFFICER. I was instructed to give you a message. If you don't put an end to your counter-revolutionary activities, Lev Davidovich, we shall be forced to move you on.

He gives TROTSKY *a letter and goes off.* TROTSKY *reads the letter. He goes to the desk and sits down heavily on the chair.* LEV SEDOV *takes the letter and reads it.*

LEV SEDOV. Letter from Alexandra. Ninth of June, nineteen twenty-eight. That was three months ago. Nina. Nina died today.

NATALIA *puts an arm round* TROTSKY's *shoulder. She remains in that position a few moments, then goes off with* LEV SEDOV. TROTSKY *rises, goes to the camp bed and lies down.*

7. ZURICH

> LENIN *is seated at back on a chair,* TROTSKY *stretched out on the camp bed.*

TROTSKY. Move you on. Move you on. Nearly ten years in exile. Cut off from events in Russia. What use is a rebel who has spent ten years abroad? We conspire together. Groups fatally split. And a year of total war. I've seen slaughter, trenches full of bloody bits of flesh, splintered bones. Heard the screaming. Looking at history from a humanitarian, from a moral, standpoint leads nowhere, I know. But shows we are still crawling about in an epoch of savage barbarism. Science. Such hopes we had. Everything now, everything serving destruction. Is this the pre-revolutionary era? Pathological bigwigs. Unctuous priests. Highwaymen, confidence tricksters in parliament. Liars and slanderers in the press. Here in Zurich, passing through, a single room, bags packed, what can we do from here to set the wheels of history in motion?

LENIN. Hm. Haven't been wasting our time. No revolutionary practice without revolutionary theory. Ten years. What are ten years? Every day, every hour I was tuned in to things going on. We worked in secret. As our people in Russia worked in underground cells. New men are coming up there. Ruthless, active. Cunning, clever. Eyes firm on the goal. These matter. The others have outlived their time. Like the German party, betraying the International and making common cause with the Kaiser, our veterans have landed themselves in the nationalistic mess on the side of the Tsar. Now do you understand why I threw out the old guard?

TROTSKY. I tried to create understanding. Wanted to bring the groups together.

LENIN. Yes, you put yourself forward as the man who stood

above the party. Neither Bolshevik nor Menshevik, but
revolutionary socialist.

TROTSKY. I wanted to bring the groups together.

LENIN. A pious wish. Cut down infighting among the socialists.
That is to say, deny that there are differences of opinion.
Don't seek out the root causes. That is a great help – to our
enemies.

TROTSKY. I wanted to settle the conflicts, to put an end to the
confusion among the workers. To restore confidence, initiative.

LENIN. What virtue: to neutralize opposites. By trying to make
us all friends together you simply betray the workers. Who
is to be reconciled? The party and its liquidators? There's no
room for compromise.

TROTSKY. Yes, I realized the old guard had no heart for the
proletarian stage of the revolution. They didn't want to
depend on the workers, didn't want them to win. Because
they feared them. Wanted nothing more than to be the left
wing in a bourgeois democracy.

LENIN. The only active international forces are the Russian
workers' groups that support us. The revolutionary vanguard.
The army doesn't yet know its own strength. Many soldiers
won't see it even at the moment of decision. We must take
our propaganda, our agitation to the front, into the trenches.
In the west as well. Turn this imperialistic war into a socialist
revolution. Point its weapons not against the wage slaves of
other countries, but against its own governments.

TROTSKY. On that at least we agree. That we must continue
the struggle, even if it leads to Russia's military defeat. Not
wait any more for another country to begin. Our initiative
will drag Europe along with it.

RADEK, RAKOVSKY, INESSA ARMAND *enter.*

INESSA. Parvus is here, Ilyich. Insists on seeing you.

RADEK. Comes among the refugees like God Almighty. To

give us alms. Living in a suite in the Baur au Lac on cham-
pagne and fat cigars. Has a harem of blonde concubines.

LENIN. That opportunist. That German socialistic chauvinist.
I won't see him. What news from Petrograd, Radek?

RADEK. No bread, no coal. But Fabergé the court jeweller is
doing a fabulous trade. Countess Vyrubova boasts she has
never bought so many clothes and jewels in a single season as
this winter. The night-clubs are stuffed with staff officers,
members of parliament, theatrical managers, ballerinas,
generals and other illustrious humbugs. It's a real orgy,
a shower of gold on a plague. The aristocrats drinking to the
muzhiks they've shipped off to fight in Galicia.

PARVUS *comes in, wearing an open fur coat, top-hat in hand.*

PARVUS. Comrade Lenin, I can help you to mobilize a hundred thousand Russian workers and call out a general strike.

LENIN. We don't work with agents of the German government.

PARVUS. You know I support the Russian revolution.

LENIN. As imperialists now and again support revolutionaries
and national liberation movements. Even rebellion can be
made to yield profits.

PARVUS. Vladimir Ilyich, you should be able to appreciate my
tactics. I'm exploiting the situation in imperial Germany.
Capitalism shall be invited to dig its own grave.

LENIN. I know your plans, Parvus. A niche for yourself as
reformer and saviour of the Russian revolution. Go away.
Tell your foreign ministry we are not for sale.

PARVUS. If you imagine the German proletariat is thinking of
revolution, you're deluding yourself. I tell you, there'll
be no revolution in Germany as long as the war lasts. That
can happen only in Russia. I can let you have a million
roubles at once.

LENIN. Get out. Don't come near me again.

PARVUS. I despise political outcasts who starve for their ideals.
What sort of a life is this? Living in filthy rooms. In attics.

You, Lenin, sleep on top of a sausage factory. I know, the
stink of rotting flesh makes you mad. But hold on. Hold on.

PARVUS goes off. TROTSKY, *who has been lying on the camp
bed, sits up.* LENIN *comes forward.*

LENIN. Scoundrel. Traitor. An awful example of the collapse
of the second International.

RADEK *laughs.*

RADEK. Profiteer. Speculator. But he's got twenty million
Swiss francs in his pocket. We'll need him one day.

RAKOVSKY. We shouldn't mistrust him. He's smuggled a lot
of comrades through Germany. He thinks all problems can
be solved with money. Maybe he's right. He's the only one
who can help us get back home when the time comes.

LENIN. Certainly we need clever people, Rakovsky. But they
must have clean hands.

RADEK *regards his hands, laughing.*

RADEK. Have we got clean hands? Haven't we robbed mail
coaches and trains, raided banks, dispossessed tradesmen
and factory owners? Revolution eats money. Haven't we
fought side by side with bandits and sat with them in prison
cells? Did we ever ask who was with us setting traps or lay-
ing bombs? Haven't rogues and pimps and thieves gone to
the gallows singing the Red Flag? Don't the social outcasts
belong to us too? The lowest of the low? Wasn't it you,
Vladimir Ilyich, who laughed at Rosa when she complained
of the brutality we thought necessary? Remember Parvus
when we come to power, when we make treaties and alliances
with German, French, British and American super-
gangsters.

*Enter a group of writers and artists – regulars at the public
house at the corner of the Spiegelgasse, founders of the Café*

Voltaire and the Dadaists: EMMY HENNINGS, HUGO BALL, TRISTAN TZARA, MARCEL JANCO, RICHARD HUELSENBECK *and their protégée,* ANNA BLUME.

HENNINGS. All the rebels gathered in our little saloon. Radek, Lenin. And Trotsky. I hear you're still living opposite, Monsieur Lenin. Because your landlady said the soldiers must now turn their guns on their own governments. The news has got around.

BALL. Do you still believe in European culture, Trotsky? Your harmonious arches, your idealistic steeples? I've read all your edicts on art and poetry. Haven't you seen yet that all the splendid façades are cracking and crumbling?

TZARA. Tristan Tzara, that's me, and Janco, and Emmy Hennings and Hugo Ball, and Richard Huelsenbeck, and Anna Blume, the streetwalker from the corner, and Max Ernst, and Duchamp in New York. Remember these names. An International. We'll go down in history too, like you. You say bourgeois values must be destroyed, we don't want to keep any of them, they must disappear, we'll begin again. That's our programme too. We shall smash everything they built up. Down with the Venus de Milo. Down with the Sistine Madonna. Down with statues, temples, libraries, museums. Down with all this muck on pedestals, in frames, in glass cases. All lies. All hypocrisy. The real voice, that is heard in the clatter of the tanks, the rattle of shrapnel, the throbbing of aeroplanes. Groans, death-rattles, farts, belches, howls. That is our language. Music? Is there still a place for music? Who listens to music with a knife in his ribs, a bullet in his guts?

HUGO BALL *climbs on a chair.*

BALL. You must join hands with us, you rationalists, you revolutionary technicians. You bring down the despots, the bloodsuckers in the banks and factories. We bring down the

bosses who keep our impulses, our imagination, under lock
and key. From the ruins the downtrodden working slave,
the starved court jester will rise and generate an almighty
force. We must unite. We, the unpredictable, emotional
artists and you, the planners, the designers. Undivided. Or
our revolution will trickle away into the sand. New man
must be a creator. New art is life. Breathing is art. Movement is art. We swim in the air. We fly. Life is flying.

*He jumps from the chair with outstretched arms and falls
flat. He is helped to his feet amid laughter.* TROTSKY *rises
from the camp bed.*

ANNA BLUME. I don't know what he means. Vladimir Ilyich
told me that after the revolution the libraries and museums
will belong to us, and the palaces and the theatres. So why
should they be destroyed? Then they won't be any use to us
any more.

JANCO. We don't need them. They were made only for the
people up top, those who spit on your head. To whom you
sold yourself by the hour. As we all do.

ANNA BLUME. But I want to see them. I want to go inside.

LENIN. Yes. These things have split society. Yes. They have
served the ruling class. But we have learnt to make use of
them. We have gained knowledge from them. They have
helped us to develop skills. To go beyond our limits. The
pseudo-revolutionaries, they can afford to destroy our cultural heritage. They have had more than their fill of it. But
we, we still need it. We wish to take it over whole. The
people who have so far been cut off from it, they shall decide
what is to be thrown out, what can still be used.

HENNINGS. Nothing. Nothing can still be used. Not even by
you, Anna. We must learn everything afresh. Bla bla bla. Da
da da. Dada. That's what the new art will be called. Anti-
art. Born in the Spiegelgasse in Zurich. In the Café Voltaire.
In the year of blood. In the month of the spilling guts. On

the day of the death scream. To the world. To the public of the world. The new culture, Dada, is born. Da da. Da da da. To the people of the future. To the visionaries. Let your clothes rot on your bodies. Dress yourselves in your own hair. Come and go like rain and fog. Da da. Da da da.

ANNA BLUME. What's she talking about, Inessa? Has she gone off her head?

BALL. No. She is the mouthpiece of the higher reason. Reason freed from the yoke of precedents and laws.

TROTSKY. We imagined once that the world would be governed by conscious knowledge, by critical thinking. But throughout history consciousness has tottered along behind the facts. To that extent you are right.

LENIN *is suddenly violently angry. All turn to him in concern.*

LENIN. And just because human intelligence is so puny, for the very reason that it is so puny, that is why I shall never permit its weak glow to be extinguished.

A moment of silence. LENIN *walks agitatedly to and fro.*

TROTSKY. All these great happenings everywhere. These shocks and upsets. They must produce a new form of art. A change in the social pattern must free the artist too from his old restraints.

HUELSENBECK. It will be a shock course. Things irrational, things so far concealed, things never before defined in words and symbols shall find expression.

TROTSKY. But not in an ecstatic, mystical way. Art must help to change the world. An art freed from the clutches of agents, speculators, profiteers. The new art which belongs to all must serve the revolution.

HUELSENBECK. And return to captivity? Art must belong to nobody but itself.

LENIN. Art has no right to absolute freedom. Art must take sides. We shall come down heavily against artistic self-sufficiency. Against any sort of ridicule, vulgarity, cynicism, hate directed against us under the cloak of creative genius.

HUELSENBECK. You take art much too seriously. You still believe in the great works.

TROTSKY. One single great work. Produced collectively. It will come. First in a vast muddle of stylistic experiments, exaggerations, aberrations. Much of it formless, flat, rough, inexpert. Echoes of the past. Utopian dreams. Most of it worthless, quickly thrown aside. But within it we shall see the path along which new man is progressing.

INESSA. But who's to judge whether it is revolutionary art? Who decides what is harmed and what is helped by it? Where is the limit? Who decides where to intervene?

LENIN. The proletariat will fix the standards.

RAKOVSKY. And what will the proletariat say to our progressives? Have you seen the pictures of Malevich, Kandinsky, Chagall, Tatlin, Lissitzky? Do you know the poems of Blok, of Mayakovsky? And all the things happening in the theatre? Meyerhold, Vakhtangov, Tairov. Will the workers see that as revolutionary art?

LENIN. Once libraries, museums, schools, universities are in the hands of the people, a proletarian culture will emerge, and with it proletarian art. And since the workers will want to study, to learn, to explore, to educate themselves, they will expect a lot from their artists. They will have no taste for empty magic. Their art will be realistic and scientific.

TROTSKY. What we are visualizing, what is already beginning to emerge, will that ever be proletarian culture? Can there be a proletarian culture at all? Before us years of revolution, civil war, bitter class warfare. Art will join in the fight, yes. But the proletariat, it will need all its strength, to seize power, to maintain it and use it. Culture will mean to start with hundreds of millions of people learning to read and write and do their sums. In a socialist society the proletariat

will cease to be the proletariat. The revolution will put an
end to class culture. What will come is mass art, communal
art, that is to say, classless art.

TRISTAN TZARA *pulls* ANNA BLUME *to the back.*

TZARA. Brothers, sisters. Let us storm the marble halls, the
crematoria of the spirit. Out with the starch-shirted busts,
the laurel wreaths. In with the roofless. The armless, the
legless.
BALL. The headless.

ANNA BLUME *turns towards* LENIN.

ANNA BLUME. Ilyich. Ilyich.

She is pulled off by TRISTAN TZARA. *The whole group
follows them, laughing and imitating trumpet calls.* INESSA
ARMAND, RADEK *and* RAKOVSKY *join them. All go off.
Only* LENIN *and* TROTSKY *remain.* LENIN *presses his
temples with both hands.*

TROTSKY. The doctor ordered you rest. Relaxation. Walks.
LENIN. Hm. Holidays? We need every hour.

LENIN *goes to the camp bed and lies down.*

Haven't time now even to listen to Inessa playing. The
Appassionata. Ha. Ha ha ha. What wonderful things human
beings can think up. But I can't listen. Music affects the
nerves. One wants to say nice sweet things, stroke people's
hair. Ha. Ha ha ha. To think such beautiful thoughts, while
they are living in hell. I can't bear it. No, stroke them, and
they bite off your hand. Beat them on the head, that's what
one must do.
TROTSKY. Vladimir Ilyich, one must relax sometimes. When
were you in Copenhagen with Inessa Armand? How many
years ago?
LENIN. In nineteen ten. September. For ten days.

TROTSKY. And that is all?

LENIN *laughs*.

LENIN. Piano-playing. A walk. A hotel room. That sort of thing is quickly over. Leaves no traces.

TROTSKY. Live just for the revolution. Day and night. Firm. Clear. Spotless. Exemplary.

LENIN. The work must be done. (*He puts his hands to his head.*)

TROTSKY. You had no sleep last night, I know. Yet up in the morning laughing. Ha ha ha, how are you, what's new? How do you do it? I know your nerves are upset. Chest, hips. Your whole body inflamed. Rashes. Eczema. How can you stand it?

LENIN. It's not important.

TROTSKY. Not important? The body. Feel it all the time. Stomach. Intestines. Heart. Kidneys. These functions often claim my attention for days on end. Growing old. The beginning of death. Time. I thought of that even as a child. Saw it once as something long, like the stone step outside the house. Chronology. Counting. Time is formless. Has no shape till you begin to count. Sometimes I wake up sobbing. Terribly disturbed. Like falling through a strange door. Into a room you don't know. An odd light. Echoing voices. This searching for connections. Books. Unknown words. References you don't understand. Everything at times like on a huge stage. When I first went to a theatre, Ilyich, it was overwhelming. Indescribable. Out of my mind nearly at what was going on. Sat through all the intervals in case I might miss something. Afterwards they asked me: what did you see? I couldn't say. What had I seen? What had I seen?

> LENIN *is lying motionless on the camp bed. Four soldiers come in, as before, dressed in Red Army uniform. They march to the bed, lift* LENIN *up and carry him off at back.*

8. TWENTY-FIFTH OF OCTOBER

*A crowd of workers, sailors, soldiers come slowly forward.
Torn clothing, muddy military coats, head-scarves, heavy fur
caps, rifles on shoulders, belts with ammunition pouches.
They take* TROTSKY *up in their midst and lead him forward.*

TROTSKY. There in their houses, there they're sitting now.
The bourgeoisie. Huddled together. Listening. Trying to
guess what is happening in the dangerous streets. Officials
still writing out regulations which will never be read again.
Schoolchildren sitting over books long out of date. Poets
sweating on verses which no one will read. Not a sound.
They expected barricades. Fires. Looting. Streams of blood.
But all is quiet. They can't understand it. Why is everything
so terribly quiet? There they sit. Before us. Slowly we have
crept up on them. They don't yet know. We needed no loud
calls to bring us together. We've come from the workshops,
the factories. From the ships. From the front. They pant, and
sweat a little. But prefer not to see us yet. They can't accept
that we, who always stood at the back, miles behind, invis-
ible, we are now at the front, right on top of them. We have
been preparing. For years. Now we are showing ourselves.
We shall force them to see us. They start to tremble.

*The gathering moves slowly back. A part goes off. Others
remain as sentries, messengers, members of the Red Guard.
A few stretch out on the floor to sleep. A telephone is manned.
Bread and sausages are brought, a can of tea.*
Enter LENIN, DZERZHINSKY, KAMENEV, RAKOVSKY,
SVERDLOV, SMIRNOV, SHLYAPNIKOV, POZNANSKY,
MRACHKOVSKY. TROTSKY *sits down at one edge of the desk,*
LENIN *at the other. There is a constant coming and going.
Notes are written, handed over. Soldiers, sailors come in
with reports, go off with orders.*

DZERZHINSKY. The aristocratic daughters of Smolny never dreamed that the revolution would be led from here. On the door outside it says 'Class mistress'.

FIRST SOLDIER. Now there's another class here.

TROTSKY. How are the occupations going, Dzerzhinsky?

DZERZHINSKY. The Kexholm regiment is holding the telegraph office. Two men at the main counter. That was enough. The clerks saw who's in charge now.

TROTSKY. The telephone exchange?

FIRST SAILOR. A proper racket when we got there with our troops. Telephone girls in hysterics, waving their arms. What's the matter, girls, d'you think we want to shoot you? You can all go. We can work it by ourselves. And off they went. The whole Morskaya street full of screeching hats and coats.

Laughter. A soldier goes to MRACHKOVSKY.

MRACHKOVSKY. Electricity works, water works, main post office, all secured. Reliable guards.

SECOND SAILOR. The *Aurora* is now at anchor at the Nikolaevsky Bridge. We've let the bridge down. Secured the crossing. A few tanks about. No sign of the junkers.

TROTSKY. How are things at the Peter and Paul Fortress?

SECOND SAILOR. They've got eighty machine-guns. Control the quay and the Troizky Bridge. A few comrades out stirring things up in the bicycle batallion. Typical people on wheels, most of them from the upper regions.

SHLYAPNIKOV. We've taken the railway stations without a shot fired. The pioneers were there. Slid off once it got dark. Bubnov's in contact with the railway workers. Miliutin is seeing the food supplies through.

TROTSKY. And the state bank?

DZERZHINSKY. Detachment of marines, forty men, on their way.

LENIN. And there are comrades among us who have publicly

declared that it was too soon for an armed rising. Who think we should wait for the Soviet Congress tomorrow. As if rebellion were a matter of votes.

KAMENEV. So far we've always stuck firm to the principle that party policy follows the majority vote.

LENIN. To wait for an uncertain vote now, Kamenev, would be a betrayal of the revolution. Opportunities for armed rising must be seized as they come. You can't keep them for later. History gives no pardon to revolutionaries who put off till tomorrow what they can win today.

KAMENEV. Zinoviev and I are not the only ones who think an armed rising now endangers not only the party but the whole Russian and international revolution.

LENIN. We have held back the order to attack long enough. The masses are demanding it now. They have no more time for doubters and neutralists. The proletariat is on the move throughout Europe. The German navy in revolt. The Italian socialists rising. The whole world situation hangs in the balance.

KAMENEV. The German naval revolt is a significant symptom. But it's not active support for the Russian revolution. We have never said revolution in Russia depends only on the working class. A majority of the workers and the armed forces on our side is not enough. There's still the huge mass of lower middle class. The party must first be given a chance to grow. The people must clearly see what it's trying to do.

LENIN. Abandon the workers now and they'll turn from us, as they did from the Mensheviks and the Social Revolutionaries. Unless they're led, they'll dissipate their forces. Convulsive movements. Anarchistic outbreaks. Desperate partisan battles. The bourgeoisie both here and throughout the world will use the breathing space to smash our organization. The success of our revolution hangs now from a day or two of fighting.

SHLYAPNIKOV. To hear you talk, comrades, you'd think our

rebellion needs excusing. No one asked permission when we began in the metal factory last February. That was a workers' revolt. And a workers' and soldiers' revolt is what it still is. We're giving nothing more away.

FIRST WORKER (*to telephone operator*). Come on, we're waiting. Still no news from the arms factory? The Red Guard needs rifles.

TELEPHONE OPERATOR. I'm through now. You can go down. Five thousand rifles with ammunition boxes. Get a requisition from Trotsky.

Two heavily armed sailors enter.

THIRD SAILOR. We've occupied the state bank.

RAKOVSKY. The holiest of holies.

THIRD SAILOR. A section of Kadets at the Yekaterinsky Canal. Just goggled when they saw us. We've been sent to guard the bank, we said. They let us through without lifting a finger. So in we went. The doors weren't even locked. We put a guard on every phone.

FOURTH SAILOR. You should have seen the bank people. Where have you got your gold? Just a little tap with a bayonet and they whipped out the keys. Then down the stairs to the vaults.

RAKOVSKY. And?

FOURTH SAILOR. Gold bars lying there like cakes in the oven.

RAKOVSKY. That's more than the Paris Commune dared to do.

ANTONOV *enters. He reports to* TROTSKY. LENIN *meanwhile consults papers and makes notes.*

ANTONOV. The Winter Palace is surrounded. Blockade closing in on the Admiralty Quay, Nevsky Prospect, Mars Field, Palace Quay. We're stationed at the railings and moats of the Hermitage. All gates to the Palace Gardens in our hands. We advanced to the main entrance, disarmed the guards. The Kadets have entrenched themselves behind wooden stakes.

Firewood. Have received reinforcements. A women's batallion. The *Aurora*'s waiting for a signal from the fortress. Blanks first, as agreed. Then, if necessary, fire.

TROTSKY. Kamenev's and Zinoviev's declaration could be useful to us. It'll strengthen Kerensky's opinion that we're not yet ready to strike, are willing to negotiate. Our tactics so far have been to make all our preparations look like security measures. Against a counter-revolution from the right. All we need now, Antonov, is an act of provocation. Then attack becomes defence.

ANTONOV. In the palace they're reeling around like hypnotized chickens. We sent up patrols from the cellars. The government's taken refuge in the throne room. Behind each one an old footman in livery, filling up glasses.

A female worker and a printing worker come in hurriedly.

FEMALE WORKER. We were printing off *Pravda* when a troop of junkers came in. They swept the galleys off the table with their rifles, smashed the matrices. We were forced out, the doors locked and sealed. Give us an armed escort and we promise to get the paper out.

TROTSKY. Officials seals on the doors of the Bolshevik newspaper. The signal for battle. Immediate order to the Litovsk regiment. A company to protect the workers' press.

PRINTING WORKER. Get some from the sixth pioneer batallion too. They're neighbours, good friends of ours.

TROTSKY *writes some notes and gives them to a messenger.*

TROTSKY. Antonov, raise the red lantern on the Peter and Paul Fortress.

ANTONOV *goes off.*

Poznansky, write this down. Order Number One. The Petrograd Soviet is in danger. Counter-revolutionary rioters, junkers and assault troops are preparing an offensive.

Take up action stations and await further instructions. Disobedience or delay in carrying out orders will be regarded as betrayal of the revolutionary cause.

POZNANSKY *gives the written order to a soldier, who goes off with it.*

LENIN. Control of the press. The idea of dispensing with that comes from the same sort of people who think a coalition with the Mensheviks and the Social Revolutionaries still possible. What nonsense these democrats talk, even the most left-wing ones, about the freedom of the press. Why do the liberals want a free press? So they can slander us. The right to speak is less important than the right to live. First thing is to establish proletarian dictatorship over the press. The press is a weapon in the revolutionary struggle. All moral considerations must take second place.

SMIRNOV. In the city centre, right beside the palace, people are out taking walks. It's unbelievable. The trams are running as usual, the restaurants are open, and the cinemas and theatres. I've just come from the Moyka. Walking around among the officers, coachmen, ladies dressed up in their finery, it made me feel like a dwarf trying to move a mountain. And on my way here I had my coat stolen. I thought at first it was a patrol. It was just a few youngsters.

TROTSKY. Where was that, Smirnov?

SMIRNOV. Here, just outside Smolny. They came up to me and said, Comrade, take your fur coat off, it's warmed you long enough, we're freezing. Quick, they said, off with it. I had to give it them.

Laughter.

TROTSKY. Poznansky, get this out immediately. All people creating disorder, looting, knifing or shooting in the streets of Petrograd will be tried by court martial and, if found guilty, summarily executed.

DZERZHINSKY. Just look at us. Grey faces. Unshaven. We'll lose the revolution if we don't get some sleep. Oh, for a bath, a clean shirt.

A female worker in a soldier's greatcoat brings in a bowl of water and puts it down before DZERZHINSKY. *He washes his face, fills his mouth with water, gargles, spits it out.* LENIN *rises, walks to and fro.*

LENIN. So soon after persecution, exile – power. It makes one giddy. (*He makes a circular movement with a hand around his head.*) We must form a government. What shall we call ourselves? Not on any account ministers. Vile word.

SVERDLOV. Commissars, perhaps? But there are too many commissars already.

SMIRNOV. Chief Commissars. Or People's Commissars.

LENIN. People's Commissars. Hm. And the government as a whole?

TROTSKY. Soviet. Soviet of course. Soviet of People's Commissars.

LENIN. People's Commissars. Excellent. Smells frightfully of revolution. As chairman of the Council of People's Commissars I propose Comrade Trotsky.

TROTSKY. I beg leave to decline.

SVERDLOV. Trotsky was too long outside the party. He's been with us only a few months.

LENIN. There are no better Bolsheviks than Trotsky. He stands at the head of the Petrograd Soviet. I state this categorically. There are no official records of these days. Only scribbled notes and verbal orders. None of us has time to write history. Who knows how many of us will still be here in the next weeks, months? Those who follow us will report incompletely, perhaps misrepresent. I put on record that Comrade Trotsky planned every step of the rebellion. He led the Petrograd Soviet to victory.

TROTSKY. I would rather stay outside the government. Look after the party press.

LENIN. Take the Commissariat for Internal Affairs. The fight against the counter-revolution is now the main task.

TROTSKY. Shall we give the enemy the extra weapon of saying I am a Jew?

LENIN. We are engaged in a great international revolution. What do such trifles matter?

TROTSKY. Maybe the revolution is great. But there are still fools enough about.

LENIN. Must we do things to suit them?

SMIRNOV. Lev Davidovich should be set to tackle Europe. He knows it. He should take over foreign affairs.

LENIN. Do you accept Smirnov's suggestion?

TROTSKY. With reluctance. What's there to do? I'll issue a few revolutionary proclamations to the peoples of the world and then shut up shop.

A SAILOR *in dirty uniform enters.*

SECOND SAILOR. In the Peter and Paul Fortress the officer cadets first said they couldn't fire the guns. Rusted, compressors not oiled. And the crews vanished. Then a few marine artillerymen came up. No experience, but good Bolsheviks. They got the guns ready, can fire without oil. We couldn't find a red lantern. Lost a lot of time looking for one. But found it in the end. It's up. The *Aurora* has answered.

TROTSKY. Did you shoot?

SECOND SAILOR. Not necessary. The Winter Palace is ours.

TROTSKY. Is that confirmed?

TELEPHONE OPERATOR. Not yet. But Kerensky has bolted.

SECOND SOLDIER. The women are still under cover.

SVERDLOV. Comrades, in a few hours the congress will begin. Let's go into the chamber. Get things organized.

Most go off. Only LENIN *and* TROTSKY *remain at front.
At back the telephone operator, and now and again messengers coming and going.* LENIN *lies down on the camp bed.*
TROTSKY *stretches out on a row of chairs near him. A
female worker puts a few military coats over them.*

LENIN. The people in the town still think the workers are
incapable of running the state machinery. The old machinery. As if that were important. The machinery won't be
taken over, nor adapted. It will be smashed. And what we
put in its place, every worker will be able to run that.

9. TWENTY-SIXTH OF OCTOBER

TROTSKY. Yet all the same. Far too few workers in the
government ranks. Far too many intellectuals, orators.

LENIN. You mistrust the party leadership?

TROTSKY. Vladimir Ilyich, you know your decisions are
accepted by everybody. Sverdlov, Rykov, Bukharin, most of
the others, they couldn't believe their ears when you talked
in May of a proletarian revolution, no longer a middle-class
democratic one. Many thought you'd gone mad, that exile
had robbed you of your sense of reality.

LENIN. Said I'd become a Trotskyist. Ha. Ha ha ha.

TROTSKY. They jibbed for a while. Then came over to the
new course. Kamenev, Zinoviev. We threatened to expel
them, they threatened to resign. But they stayed on. All of
them. Unity was preserved. The group leadership works.
Because you are there. And because behind it is the real
power. The workers, the soldiers.

LENIN. You think, if the White Guards were to kill you and
me, the party would collapse?

TROTSKY. Let's hope they don't kill us.

LENIN. But if we weren't here? Do you think without us the
October Revolution could never have taken place?

They lie a few moments in silence. SVERDLOV *comes in and looks at them, then withdraws.*

TROTSKY. Sometimes I think so. Sometimes not. In February the monarchy was simply swept away. In a huge outburst of energy. No leadership then. After that the short period of bourgeois rule. A provisional government with no links to the people. New initiatives from below. Isolated actions. Self-help. Setting up of advisory councils. Now we come along. Our achievement: to bring the innumerable spontaneous actions together. To merge them into the Bolshevik effort. We have the overall vision. See the immediate possibilities. Put into concrete form what was present in the raw. Restrict ourselves to a single military operation. Carried out by a limited number of Red Guards. The masses are not fighting now. Only the proletariat *avant-garde*. How many of us are there? Five thousand, ten thousand. History will remember the names of a few dozen. The millions of the nameless are now asking: will we do justice to all their efforts?

LENIN. And the quarrel between us? Over now?

TROTSKY. Was it a quarrel? Not rather a mutual testing of strength? We pushed each other forward. Took over each other's ideas. Ironed out differences of opinion. The revolution was still untried. Different views and possibilities had to clash and be proved in practice. In the future too there'll be controversy, contradictions. Would we be Marxists otherwise?

LENIN. Ha. Ha ha ha. My rage against you was often violent. Because you weren't one of us. Because you held fast to those false humanists. Were you trying to outplay me, perhaps? To grab the leadership yourself?

TROTSKY. Maybe the impulse was there. Somewhere in me there's still that poor young Jewish lad Lev Bronstein from Yanofska. This fantastic urge for power and influence. Difficult to appreciate that none of it exists for you.

Ambition. The need to prove oneself. None of it exists for you.

LENIN. We are worthy of each other. But I've got only a few more years. There are times now when for an hour or so I am gone, blotted out. The others, they won't put up with you when I'm no longer here. Your self-assurance, your international interests. They'll call it arrogance, vanity. They'll band together and throw you out. Then we'll see what the revolutionary masses are worth. Whether they'll come out on your side.

Machine-gun fire. Enter the participants at the All-Russian Congress, among them SVERDLOV, SMIRNOV, KAMENEV, ZINOVIEV, DZERZHINSKY, RYKOV, RAKOVSKY, SHLY-APNIKOV, MRACHKOVSKY, MARTOV, KHINCHUK, ABRAMOVICH, ARKADI KREMER, DEUTSCH, KUCHIN, PETERSON. *They sit down at and around the desk. It is a large gathering. A babble of voices.* TROTSKY, LENIN, KAMENEV, SVERDLOV *sit at the middle of the desk. A soldier gives* TROTSKY *a message.*

TROTSKY. In the name of the military revolutionary committee I declare that the provisional government has ceased to exist.

Cheers and protests.

Kerensky has fled from the Winter Palace in an American embassy car. He has left the capital. Some ministers have been arrested. Others will be arrested in the next few hours. We are about to take the Winter Palace.

Applause. Uproar.

KHINCHUK. Take care of the palace. It mustn't be stormed.
VOICE. The Winter Palace is in ruins.
FIRST SAILOR. There are no ruins. Only warning shots. That was enough. Get on with your work, comrades.
MARTOV. You have decided the matter of power through a

conspiracy. The various revolutionary parties are presented with a *fait accompli*. The crisis can only be solved peacefully by setting up an authority which can be recognized by all democratic forces.

SHLYAPNIKOV. Not a conspiracy, Martov. An armed rising of the workers and soldiers of Petrograd.

MARTOV. The congress cannot meet under threat of arms.

KHINCHUK. There must be talks with the provisional government.

ABRAMOVICH. Abolish the constituent assembly and there'll be chaos. Russia will be plunged into civil war.

TROTSKY. With whom are we to negotiate? I say, with whom? With the people who are moving out? In this congress millions of workers and peasants are represented. Are these to negotiate on equal terms with that miserable heap whom nobody in Russia supports?

ABRAMOVICH. You don't represent the whole people.

RYKOV. We represent the people that matter. We Bolsheviks represent the proletariat of both town and country.

MARTOV. We demand an immediate cease-fire on both sides. We demand the setting up of a united democratic front.

Catcalls. Laughter. Applause.

VOICE. Are you Mensheviks still here?

LENIN. If there are any comrades here who don't accept our programme, they had better disappear with the other deserters and compromisers. Let's get on. Next point.

MARTOV, ABRAMOVICH, KHINCHUK *spring to their feet.*

MARTOV. This congress is unconstitutional.

Laughter. Uproar. The right wing of the Mensheviks begin to withdraw.

KAMENEV. Put in the minutes: Martov, Abramovich, Khinchuk leave the chamber with the right-wing Mensheviks.

A clerk writes. TROTSKY *calls after the departing men.*

TROTSKY. You're bankrupt. Your role's played out. Go where you belong – into the rubbish bins of history.

Laughter. Applause. A few more delegates jump up.

KREMER. Under these conditions it is impossible for the delegates of the United Jewish Workers to take part in the debate.

KAMENEV. Put in the minutes: the delegates of the United Jewish Workers leave the chamber.

KUCHIN. Political adventurers are here deciding over the life of the nation. The soldiers in the trenches are not on your side.

Protests. PETERSON, *a soldier, rises.*

PETERSON. Who are you speaking for, Kuchin?

KUCHIN. For our people at the front. We refuse to accept any responsibility for the consequences of this gamble.

PETERSON. Enough hot air. You do *not* represent the frontline. I've just come from there. We're waiting impatiently for the soviets to assume power. Delegates who haven't been sent here by anybody should leave the congress.

Applause. KUCHIN *goes off. Some other delegates accompany him.*

KAMENEV. What's your name, comrade?

PETERSON. Peterson. Soldier from Latvia.

KAMENEV. On the minutes. The delegates of the front line army committee leave the chamber. The group of Right Social Revolutionaries leave the chamber.

Uproar. Applause. Whistling. A workers' delegation comes in.

FIRST WORKER. Comrades, you must do something about Kaledin. At once. He's trying to cut off the coalmines in the Don basin and block the food supplies.

SECOND WORKER. Kerensky's in Gatchina. He's ordered a forced march on Petrograd by the Cossack regiment.

TROTSKY *writes notes and gives them to messengers. He turns to* SHLYAPNIKOV *and* MRACHKOVSKY.

TROTSKY. Reinforcements for Miliutin. To the goods yard. To the market.

SHLYAPNIKOV *and* MRACHKOVSKY *go off. A* SAILOR *comes in.*

SECOND SAILOR. The third bicycle batallion has come over to the side of the revolution.

Cheers. A MESSENGER *gives* RYKOV *a telegram.*

RYKOV. Telegram from the Twelfth Army. Sends greetings to the congress. Reports formation of a military revolutionary committee to watch over the northern front. Attempts by the provisional government to summon armed help foiled by troop resistance. The commander-in-chief of the northern front, General Cheremissov, has agreed to subordinate himself to the committee.

Cheers. A group of soldiers – Cossacks – from the front enters.

SOLDIER. We represent the echelons sent by the provisional government to Petrograd. We have decided to join the revolutionary garrison in Petrograd.

Cheers. Delegates embrace. TROTSKY *rises.*

TROTSKY. The congress puts full power in the hands of the soviets. Workers, peasants, soldiers, the future of the revolution now lies with you.

KAMENEV *rises.*

KAMENEV. Comrade Lenin.

LENIN rises amid cheers and applause. He stands bowed. Puts a hand protectively over his eyes, then supports himself with both hands on the desk.

LENIN. We shall now proceed to construct the socialist order.

Applause.

Comrades. The workers' and peasants' revolution, for which the Bolsheviks have so continually and emphatically called, is now an accomplished fact. We shall have a soviet government in which the bourgeoisie will play not the smallest part. The oppressed masses will themselves take over the leadership. The old state machinery will vanish, and in its place a new form of government will arise, created by the soviet organizations. The exploited nations of Asia, the colonized peoples wait just as passionately as the proletariat of Europe for the downfall of capitalist rule. It is the historic task of the workers and peasants of Russia to unite these forces in a world revolution. The flames of the October Revolution will develop into a raging furnace which will overtake and consume the perpetrators of this brutal war and destroy their power.

Applause.

Further. The workers' and peasants' government, based on the soviets of workers', peasants' and soldiers' deputies, calls on all the warring nations to start immediate negotiations for a just and democratic peace. A continuation of the war, which helps the strong and wealthy nations to divide the weak conquered countries up among themselves, is, in the eyes of our government, the greatest possible crime against humanity. A condition of peace must be that equal rights are guaranteed to all countries without exception.

Applause.

The workers' and peasants' government abolishes secret
diplomacy and pledges itself to publish the contents of all
existing secret treaties. Everything in these treaties granting
special advantages and privileges to Russian landowners and
industrialists will be at once annulled. The rights of private
ownership of land will be abolished for ever.

Applause.

Further. In order to set negotiations going, the workers' and
peasants' government proposes an immediate armistice. We
appeal in particular to the class-conscious workers of the
three most advanced nations, Great Britain, France and
Germany, in the firm conviction that these will take decisive
steps to help us achieve peace, and with that to secure freedom from slavery for all.

Prolonged applause.

ZINOVIEV. All who agree with Comrade Lenin's proposals,
raise your hands.

> *All rise. From the sides soldiers and sailors come in. They all
> raise their arms and clench their fists. They begin to sing the
> 'Internationale'.*
> *As they are singing, a troop of soldiers dressed in the uniform
> of the late twenties clear themselves a path through the
> assembled people. They come up behind* TROTSKY. *Two
> officers take him by the arms. The song ends. All turn away
> from* TROTSKY. *Only* LENIN *remains standing beside him.
> One of the officers reads from a paper. All stand motionless.*

OFFICER. Citizen Trotsky, Lev Davidovich, charged under
paragraph fifty-eight/ten of the penal code with having taken
part in counter-revolutionary activity through the organization of an illegal anti-Soviet party, whose efforts have lately
been directed towards provoking anti-Soviet actions and preparing for an armed struggle against Soviet power. Resolved

that Citizen Trotsky, Lev Davidovich, be deported from the territories of the Soviet Republic. Promulgated on the twentieth of January, nineteen hundred and twenty-nine.

The officers and soldiers drag TROTSKY *towards the back. He resists. They lift him up bodily and carry him to the back.* LENIN *remains alone at the desk. Nobody looks round at the group.*

Act Two

The setting is the same.

10. KRONSTADT

> TROTSKY *is seated on a chair at front. He is looking through a telescope, describing with it a semi-circle to front. At back* LEV SEDOV *and* BLUMKIN. BLUMKIN *is talking softly,* LEV SEDOV *putting questions and making notes.* NATALIA *comes past with a large bunch of flowers.*

TROTSKY. Eternal blue sea. Eternal sun. Sea of Marmara. Homer's sea. Odysseus on Prinkipo. Rowing. Fishing. Time for study and writing. One unending holiday. Appalling. (*He opens a book.*) Do you know what he calls me, this great warrior of the British Empire? 'The ogre of Europe.'

> *He laughs and turns towards the back.* BLUMKIN *comes forward.*

He fumed, growled, snarled, bit and plotted. So writes Churchill. He raised the poor against the rich. He raised the penniless against the poor. But then the low communist criminals he had installed stood together, and put him outside.

> *Laughter.* LEV SEDOV *comes forward with a newspaper.*

LEV SEDOV. And in Berlin they write: Trotsky might be thinking of coming to Germany. We'll keep a watchful eye on him, the Jewish bloodhound.

> *Laughter.*

TROTSKY. Over there Europe. Beyond the blue sea. Beneath the burning sun. What, are they mounting the barricades?

Nothing. Not a sign. Blumkin, what have they got there except blackshirts and brownshirts?

BLUMKIN. The German party is isolated. Settling down to hibernate. Fascism's not the enemy, but the Social Democrats. Your call to the party to join with the Social Democrats is considered further proof of your treachery.

TROTSKY. We must form a common front, or the workers' movement will be ruined, for years to come. Catastrophic how people still underestimate the fascists. When we've seen them coming since nineteen-five. Even in those days the rulers weren't content with their regular armies alone. They needed hordes of filthy thugs to defend them, so brutal had their methods become. The Black Hundreds. Petty bourgeois outcasts. Discredited scholars, retired officers, rootless youngsters. Embittered. Credulous. Desperadoes. Rolling down the workers in the name of capitalism, crushing them.

BLUMKIN. At home people are saying the purpose of Trotsky's internationalism is to keep the world in a state of perpetual unrest. Why can't he understand we must first industrialize and collectivize our own country before we can think of helping others, they ask. Trotsky thinks we'll be forced to give in to the bourgeoisie if there's not a world revolution soon. But it's he who's helping the bourgeoisie and nobody else, by opposing us and refusing to trust our proletariat, our peasants to wield their power independently. Most of the opposition share that view. Pyatakov, Smirnov, Mrachkovsky, Radek – none of them support you. They've all come to terms with the party.

TROTSKY. Not Radek. He's too much of a European, a Marxist. A quarter of a century of revolutionary activity behind him. He's just been trying again to have me recalled.

BLUMKIN. Radek? I can hear him laughing. Me make a fuss about Trotsky's expulsion? I've finished with Lev Davidovich. Once and for all. We're political enemies now.

TROTSKY. That's just his tactics.

BLUMKIN. Rakovsky's the only one. But what can he do? A sick man, constant heart attacks. The opposition knows what we've got is not a proletarian democracy. But it lives in hopes of mass pressure from below. They all know, among the people they've got no support at all. It's only inside the party they can do anything.

TROTSKY. Building up the power of the state instead of building socialism. They think international revolution can be based on the Five Year Plan.

BLUMKIN. Look, Lev Davidovich. Bukharin, Zinoviev, Kamenev, they wriggle, they draw back from the coercive measures. But then they are always ready to give in, to make excuses. I've seen Zinoviev shivering and whining, frightened they'll send him back to Siberia for daring to criticize. And Bukharin, who once egged on the kulaks to grab what they could, now he shouts loudest of all: death to the kulaks. Smirnov, Mrachkovsky, who feared nothing and nobody during the civil war, both now singing the praises of the leadership, to keep in favour. And then there's this huge wave of enthusiasm sweeping the country. All force seems justified. Twenty-six million small farmers snatched from their archaic misery. Wooden ploughs replaced by squadrons of tractors and combine harvesters. Factories, reservoirs, springing up like mushrooms. Railways, armaments, planes, tanks built. Whoever utters a word against it all is blown away like thistledown.

LEV SEDOV. It's already cost the country fifteen million cows, four million horses, seven million pigs and forty million sheep.

BLUMKIN. There'll be more losses yet. They'll go to the grave along with the kulaks, who take with them whatever they can grab. And that makes people hate them all the more. Revolution has now become a struggle for the Russian soil. The epigone is an epigone no longer. Poets, film directors, painters – they all glorify him. The Omniscient Father. The Great Steersman. The Red Sun. It's all part of the general enthusiasm. He himself tries rather to damp things down. Success has gone to your head, he tells the officials when something goes wrong in the collectives. Blames them for his own mistakes. And yet it would be wrong to see him as just a tyrant. He really is convinced that he's acting in the interests of the workers' state, that he's simply safeguarding the gains of the revolution.

TROTSKY. Yes. The workers' state still exists. The conditions for building socialism still remain. There are men about who still have the revolution in their bones. But the revolution can't be contained inside one single country. It's part of a general overall development. A national form of socialism can only throw Russia back into its old primitive ways. Didn't Lenin always stress our final dependence on international revolution?

BLUMKIN. Russia is surrounded by capitalists.

TROTSKY. All the more important to break through the ring. It's exactly because the world proletariat lives in such diverse conditions, because it can't strike at the same time everywhere, that we have to keep so closely in touch. While the Soviet state is wrapping itself in isolationism, ignoring the danger in Germany, betraying the revolution in China, taking no notice of what is brewing in South America, imperialism is gathering strength.

BLUMKIN. The name of Trotsky is being scratched from the records of the revolution. In Eisenstein's film about the October rising you're not even mentioned. Coming generations will know nothing about you. History is being rewritten. And all that remains is He. From the beginning it was *he* alone who stood at Lenin's side. *He* is putting into effect what you and Lenin planned ten years ago, and what you failed to do. You tried to achieve socialism through education, by way of a cultural revolution. His way is through force, over the bodies of men. And he'll be proved right. He'll make the country so strong, industrially and militarily, that it will stand up to all attacks. You yourself, Lev Davidovich, didn't hesitate to use force when the proletarian dictatorship was threatened.

TROTSKY. Blumkin, you must not go back. You'll be put against the wall and shot when they hear you've been visiting me.

BLUMKIN. I'm an old terrorist, you know that. I couldn't be in both the GPU and the opposition at once if I didn't know how to look after myself. I can always say I visited you as a secret agent, in an attempt to make you show your hand.

> BLUMKIN *goes off.*

LEV SEDOV. He won't last long. Not even Dzerzhinsky, if he were still alive, could help him now. Blumkin was always one for desperate acts. Nineteen eighteen, when he shot the German ambassador, he could have wrecked the revolution. Wanted war to the bitter end, at any price.

TROTSKY. Terror. This idea confused many of us. We were against acts of individual terrorism. The romantic illusion of a handful of rebels wrecking tsarism with revolver shots, a knife and a few bombs. The masses were to be led towards class warfare, not invited to put their hopes in a few avengers and liberators acting on their behalf.

LEV SEDOV. And today, Father? You condemn violence and acts of sabotage against the bureaucrats?

TROTSKY. Terrorism as a method of opposition? That would be madness. The Soviet Union must be protected at all costs. Our task is to strengthen the International. To support the fight outside. (*He rises, walks to and fro.*) The only terrorism we ever recognized was the terror of the masses. It was necessary in the fight against the bourgeoisie, the Social Revolutionaries, the Mensheviks. Only with this politically based terrorism, this revolutionary force, could

the Russian proletariat, a tiny minority, come to power.
Magnificent audacity. Magnificent achievement. While the
huge mass of workers in Europe, with their powerful parties,
stood still, gave in. What was this terror, this force, against
the terror of the capitalists? But in one way we miscalcu-
lated. The class enemy did not collapse under the weight of
its own contradictions. Not yet. It gathered new strength.
Expanded unchecked. The German empire, the British
empire, they were surpassed by American capital, now busy
taking over one continent after another. The revolution?
Yes, it will go on. But in difficulties we couldn't at that time
foresee. More force will be needed before the masses can get
free of our modern imperialists. The enemy is vast. And vast
too its number of lickspittles, arse-crawlers. Mass terrorism.
Revolutionary force. Yes. Without doubt. Without hesita-
tion.

Enter the participants in talks preceding the party congress,
March 1921 : LENIN, ALEXANDRA KOLLONTAI, DZER-
ZHINSKY, PYATAKOV, SHLYAPNIKOV, RADEK *and others.*
They sit down at and near the desk. LEV SEDOV *goes off.*

LENIN. How the western world moans and groans about the
civil war and sufferings in Russia. There would have been no
civil war if the old clique hadn't resisted every step the
workers took, called in armed help from outside. The revolution itself was planned in all its phases so that it would
cost no more than a few dozen dead. They write about
hunger, need, poverty in Russia in order to frighten their
own workers. You see, that's what will happen to you if you
attempt a revolution. The glaring inequalities in their own
society they never mention. No, we don't have the wealth of
their privileged people. We haven't yet provided even the
minimum we promised. And now, when we're moving from
militant communism to a new economic phase, we have to
work from a position of isolation, a nightmare we always

feared. Comrades, we can no longer hope for a quick victory, for the victory of world revolution.

KOLLONTAI. But unrest and discontent will only increase as the days go by and still nothing is seen of the promised workers' democracy. And now new alarms, with all these purges. People are asking: why is the party expelling members in tens of thousands?

LENIN. The party must become what it once was: an *avant-garde* of the proletariat. Following the revolution we accepted too many members with unknown pasts.

DZERZHINSKY. Our tribunals are public. The personal history, the moral behaviour of every single member is being investigated. Everybody is free to speak, for or against a particular person.

SHLYAPNIKOV. That breeds denunciators, encourages selfish ambition, rivalry.

KOLLONTAI. And all the people now expelled once helped in the work of the party. Voted, put forward resolutions. Now all at once they're found incapable, unworthy. What sort of a party is that? Who can wonder if people begin to doubt it as a whole? These internal recriminations are contrary to the spirit of the cultural policy we are trying to put across.

LENIN. Comrade Kollontai. With the Cheka Dzerzhinsky directly represents the dictatorship of the proletariat. We have given him complete authority to fight the counter-revolution. We must now be able to rely on everybody. At a time when the enemy is employing all strategic means to crush us, dictatorial power is the only form of justice we can consider.

KOLLONTAI. In the communist party programme we promised categorically to abolish bureaucracy. Every Soviet member was to be employed in the administration. We advocated a constant change of job, so that members should become familiar with all aspects of the work. No specialization. The whole population was to be summoned to help.

Adaptability was the aim, a rise in the cultural level, so gradually the state machinery would be abolished. We had begun to raise a new type of human being. To rid the schools of the dead weight of discipline, outworn teaching material. To encourage independent thinking. Attack the rotten institution of family life.

VOICE. Preach free love.

KOLLONTAI. Yes, love should be enjoyed as simply as a glass of water.

VOICE. That's anti-social. What happens to the children?

KOLLONTAI. We have allowed abortion. And the young generation: they will grow up in their own communes, out of the reach of your antiquated prejudices.

LENIN. Good, Alexandra. The children of the workers and peasants are being looked after. Very good. You are encouraging revolutionary art. Putting on plays, making films. Excellent. But don't forget: behind us we have three years of civil war. The fields laid waste. More than a half of our heavy industry destroyed. The coalmines flooded. Ten million starving people. To overcome our material difficulties we need something more than Agitprop.

PYATAKOV. The proletarian revolution was victorious. But what has happened to the proletariat? In spite of bad harvests, the peasants have kept their end up. Even – since the removal of the landowners – improved it. But the little they produce they keep for themselves. Grow no surplus for the cities. The workers have hardly any bread, only a few frozen potatoes per day. Hunger drives most of them to barter, to theft, to the black market. Many who still have work in the factories steal the things they themselves produce. Now, in Spring nineteen twenty-one, we see the people who were to be the ruling class in the new state broken down and demoralized.

SHLYAPNIKOV. You don't say why, Comrade Pyatakov. It's not the workers' fault, it's the party's. The party says it represents the interests of the working class, but it only represents its own. It's trapped in its own machinery.

LENIN. I demanded your expulsion from the Central Committee, Shlyapnikov, not because you criticize, but because you carry on your criticism outside. Publish articles condemning the party. Inside the party criticism can and should be sharp. But you break the rules. If we tolerate that, the party is done for.

SHLYAPNIKOV. Comrades, the interests of the revolution are beginning to conflict with the interests of the communist party. People everywhere are saying you're more interested in consolidating your own power than in the democratic rights of the workers.

LENIN. Our state machinery is still worthless. Yes, beneath criticism. Basically still tsaristic. Just lightly greased with soviet oil. Stuffed with ancient officials who do as they please and sabotage us, consciously or unconsciously. We are gradually replacing them. But until the old machinery can be allowed to die and the workers and peasants have learnt to run an economy of the people, until then we must keep a firm grip on things.

SHLYAPNIKOV. You're trying to militarize labour. To conscript labour. Labour batallions. What sort of socialism is that? The workers see the party directives as proof of inequality. They insist that the unions and factory committees take control of the whole economy.

TROTSKY. Come down from the clouds. The workers must learn productive democratic methods before they can take control. Let's be realistic. We must work to survive. The revolution sent hundreds of thousands of men out to the battlefields. Is it not now morally entitled to send people out to rebuild the country? What do you need the unions for? To protect yourselves against the workers' state?

LENIN. It's not entirely a workers' state, Lev Davidovich. It's a workers' and peasants' state.

VOICE (BUKHARIN). What sort of state? Workers' and peasants' state?

LENIN. I hear a shout from Comrade Bukharin. Yes, and a state with bureaucratic excrescences. A pitiful label. Our state is so constructed that the proletariat still needs its organizations. Trade unions to protect the workers against the state. But also for the workers to protect our state. Trade unions, organizations of the class now in power. The ruling class. The class in which the dictatorship is embodied. Trade unions are there to educate, to recruit. A school for administrators. A school for economists. A school of communism. Next.

SHLYAPNIKOV. Yes. An instrument of education. Confronting an instrument of power. On the one side the wish for freedom, independence. On the other, coercion. That's how it looks, comrades. In Kronstadt workers and sailors are openly calling for an end to party dictatorship.

RADEK. Should we give in to the people who can't stay the course? Who no longer see where their true interests lie? The people who let reactionary groups turn them against us?

LENIN. We know their battle cries. Down with the Bolshevist tyrants. Soviets without communists. Freedom of assembly. Freedom of speech. Free elections. Vague howls for freedom, culminating in the cry: Long live the third revolution.

SHLYAPNIKOV. The workers in Petrograd and the sailors in Kronstadt are not out to restore bourgeois conditions. It was they who brought you to power. Have you forgotten that?

LENIN *springs up excitedly*.

LENIN. Not the same ones. The men who fought for the revolution are no longer here. They died for the cause. Or are today at the front. These young sailors, confused, misled, they don't know what revolution is.

TROTSKY. Shlyapnikov, you people in the workers' opposition are making a fetish of your democratic principles. You put the right to elect representatives over the rights of the party. The revolution is still fighting for its very existence. We can't yet do everything on the basis of workers' democracy.

SHLYAPNIKOV. Lev Davidovich, the crew of the *Aurora* will want to know why. The *Aurora*, which you yourself called the pride and renown of the revolution.

TROTSKY. There can be only one reply to the conspiracy of Mensheviks and anarchists against the proletarian republic. The Red Army will give it. Tukhachevsky has his orders.

KOLLONTAI. Comrade Trotsky, do we really have to tell you that we are on the side of resolute dictatorship, the dictatorship of the working class? But with the genuine co-operation of the people. Must we tell you that without the right to express opinions freely public life must wither and die? Without the help of the masses, at all levels of decision, planning becomes, must become authoritarian. Do you want to build socialism in the way the Pharaohs built the pyramids?

TROTSKY. In this uncivilized country of ours we must first train our leading people in modern methods of work. Advanced industry is still confined to the capitalist countries. We lack engineers, economists, managers. Must first achieve a balance between town and country. That we can do only by giving the peasants an economic incentive. By encouraging them to sell their surpluses, thereby profiting themselves.

VOICE (STALIN). Free trade. That's what the Mensheviks want too. The only language the kulaks understand is force.

TROTSKY. We're not yet strong enough to attack the international bourgeoisie head on. So, for the time being, we must work with them.

Signs of unrest.

Until the west is ready for revolution.

VOICE (STALIN). There's no revolutionary movement in the west. That's all pure guesswork.

TROTSKY. We shall start trade relations with the west. Encourage foreign firms to invest in us. Since their only principle is profit, they will come. And help us gain the strength to destroy them.

VOICE (STALIN). Or become capitalists ourselves.

LENIN. Yes, we shall introduce state capitalism. Not in a capitalist state, but a proletarian one. The state will hold the most important economic positions.

Signs of unrest.

TROTSKY. We shall bring competition into our industry, bonuses. Learn a lesson from American Taylorism.

VOICE (STALIN). And put an end to socialism.

LENIN. Capital is not the main enemy now. But the petty bourgeoisie, which resists state planning. We see the New Economic Policy as a contest between the socialist sector – nationalized industry, planning – and the private sector – retail trade, the rural commodity market. The proletarian state will extend the class struggle to the villages. Millions of peasants will be shown the advantages of communal farming and taught to improve their production methods. A dialectical process in which socialist patterns will gradually get the upper hand and in the end supplant the private sector.

KOLLONTAI. And the party hierarchy?

LENIN. Yes, comrade. It will disappear. No proposals that cannot be examined, amended, changed. Plebiscites. Public debates. A wide range of views. To be encouraged as the proper basis of a party which owes its existence to a gigantic popular movement. But no alliances, no splinter groups aimed at disrupting the party. Open discussion, but no organized opposition within the party. Any move in that direction must be resisted.

Enter a delegation of workers and sailors.

SAILOR. The sailors of the Baltic Fleet declare that the party

F

no longer reflects the will of its active members. The party stifles all initiative and turns all political work into paper warfare. We demand that the party return at once to democratic ways.

WORKER. The workers of Petrograd have called a general strike. They demand the election of their own works committees, union representatives and soviets, the liberation of all prisoners and the ending of the state of emergency. We are prepared to fight to the last man for our rights. Don't let it come to that.

TROTSKY jumps up.

TROTSKY. If our deluded comrades do not at once come to their senses and surrender unconditionally, they can expect no mercy from the Soviet Republic. The rebellion will be put down by force.

Some moments of silence. Then the delegation and all the participants at the meeting go off, leaving TROTSKY alone. Shots are heard.

11. THE DEATH OF LENIN

ZINAIDA VOLKOV comes in. TROTSKY turns to her.

TROTSKY. Zina?

ZINAIDA. I keep thinking of Nina. There was nothing I could do. No doctor. No medicine. She simply faded away. And now I have left Mother behind. As you did in Verkholensk. That's where it all began. We never got back our health. My first memory. Where is Father? There in bed. There you lay. A stuffed dummy. That's what you were – a stuffed dummy.

She begins to sob. TROTSKY rises and goes to her. He puts a hand on her shoulder, then begins to walk helplessly to and fro.

What a journey. In Berlin, Paris, they said: What, you are Trotsky's daughter? Why has he left? Why isn't he proud of his country? Of its terrific success? They say the Soviet Union will soon have overtaken the capitalist countries. The exploited workers of the west will soon be flooding in. Gide said to me: Why is he still grumbling, your Trotsky? I suppose he's envious because he didn't do it himself? Delegations come to Moscow to stare at the government palaces, the stations on the new metro. They're like ballrooms, I tell you, marble, candelabras, mirrors. Brecht in Berlin says only the best is good enough for them. And he's right. They're all right, Piscator and Carola Neher. But they don't know who's paying for it. They don't see the armies of forced labourers, the millions in rags, the starving, the huge prison camps. They don't see the police courts. Every day people being condemned – engineers, economists, scientists. Breakdowns in the factories blamed on sabotage, conspiracies. And behind it all – you. Insane mutterings of a Trotskyist plot. Zinoviev, Kamenev arrested. Bukharin, Smirnov, Pyatakov, Mrachkovsky all on their way back to Siberia. Mayakovsky killed himself in time. The best writers and producers are vilified. Their work labelled degenerate, formalistic, anti-socialistic. Blumkin: it's said Radek betrayed him. Yagoda ordered him to be shot. He was courageous at the end. Died shouting: Long live Trotsky. They've all been swept away, your old colleagues. Sermuks, Poznansky vanished. Glazmann hanged himself in prison. Butov: they wanted him to give false evidence, he went on hunger strike, fifty days. They just let him die. And yet, and yet – Oh, I can understand the comrades staking everything on Russia. The power the October Revolution still exerts. (*She sits down, near to collapse.*) My husband, they've taken him off too. Nina's husband liquidated. Does it distress you? Stuffed dummy. Did we ever mean anything to you? You left us to fend for ourselves. (*She springs up.*) Well, you'll soon be rid of me. And Seryosha too. Yes, Seryosha too. They've taken him to the Vorkuta.

TROTSKY. No.

ZINAIDA. I didn't mean to tell you. But you might as well know.

TROTSKY. Not Seryosha. He's never been interested in politics. He's at his institute, doing his researches.

ZINAIDA. They will finish him off. As they will finish off Lyova too. And you.

NATALIA *comes in. She embraces* ZINAIDA *and leads her to the back.*

They would take even Lenin if he were still alive. Yes, Krupskaya said that. I met her. They would fetch him and put him where he could do no harm. Krupskaya said that.

ZINAIDA *and* NATALIA *go off.* TROTSKY *goes to the desk. With pedantic thoroughness he arranges the papers on it. Then he sits for a while as at the beginning of the play.*
LENIN *enters. He walks heavily, bowed down, his head lowered. He lies down on the camp bed and presses his head with his hands.*

LENIN. We always started from the idea that you can't build socialism in a single land. We avoided too much haste in planning our industries and collectives. Always reckoned on growing support from the workers of the more advanced countries. But now there's a tendency to neglect the international programme. Bureaucracy flourishing inside the party. I ask for information, and the general secretary insolently cuts my contact to the Politburo. Says I'm too ill to bother with problems of organization. Lev Davidovich, set up a commission to cut down bureaucracy in the administration.

TROTSKY *gets up and sits down again in a chair beside the camp bed.*

TROTSKY. That wouldn't be enough. It's not only in the administration it's taken root. In the party leadership too.

LENIN. Collect the best and most experienced revolutionaries together. Set up inspectorates of workers and peasants. An examining commission with powers on a level with the leadership. We must do something before it's too late. (*He presses his temples.*) We wanted to build a workers' state. Tried to make it a living, democratic thing. We needed a centralized party to do it. And now the machine has turned against us. It's true. I try to steer, but the wheels won't respond. The vehicle swerves about in all directions. I can't control it any more. Stalin must be got out. Much too much power in his hands. He's just waiting for me to go. To grab the party for himself alone. Zinoviev, Kamenev are working with him. They always were waverers. But one mustn't judge them by their behaviour last October, they have other excellent qualities. Among the younger people Pyatakov and Bukharin would be acceptable in a collective leadership. You, Davidovich, are the most capable. But so full of ideas, you tend to extremes. Often shoot wide of the mark. Then get tangled up in administrative matters. Yes, you are partly responsible for the monolithic state that's now growing up. You see your mistakes too late.

A moment of silence. TROTSKY *sits in a sunken attitude.*

Why don't you speak? Why, when I'm about to go, do you suddenly become so weak and helpless? Why do you pull back? Why don't you accept my suggestion? Fight in my place at the party conference for the revival of proletarian democracy? Against the bureaucrats.

TROTSKY. The Politburo calls my attacks on them attacks on the party. They push the general secretary forward and don't see it is he who is pushing them.

LENIN. So you go on waiting. Your over-confidence again. Do you think they'll run after you? Proclaim you my successor?

A period of silence. LENIN *lies stretched out, an arm over his face.* TROTSKY *stands up and walks to and fro.*

TROTSKY. Beside you I could work. Could lead the fight against bureaucratic methods. I watched the new generation, the young cadres. Could talk to them. Be damned to passive obedience, servility. Stand up for your beliefs. Defend them. But when you died, all that remained was the struggle for power. I couldn't join in that.

LENIN. You mustn't let yourself be pushed aside, Lev Davidovich. You must be firm, unyielding. They'll see you're right in the end. Our revolution must spread out into world revolution, or it will die. Everything must be sacrificed to that, all short-term advantages ignored. International class warfare. Hold firm to that. China's on the brink of revolution. Russia and China. If India comes in, we'll have an overwhelming majority. Keep on. Keep on.

He lies with closed eyes, stretched out stiffly. Trotsky goes to a chair at front and sits.
Four soldiers, as before, march in towards the bed. They lift LENIN *up and carry him to the back. Figures appear there:* KAMENEV, ZINOVIEV, PYATAKOV, DZERZHINSKY, RAKOVSKY, SMIRNOV, BUKHARIN, STALIN. *The soldiers lay* LENIN *on a bier. The others lift the bier and, closely huddled, bear it towards the front with slow, dragging steps.* TROTSKY *remains motionless.*

STALIN. In leaving us, Comrade Lenin commanded us to protect the unity of our party. We swear, Comrade Lenin, to honour your command. In leaving us, Comrade Lenin ordered us to maintain and strengthen the dictatorship of the proletariat. We swear, Comrade Lenin, to honour your command. In leaving us, Comrade Lenin enjoined us to be faithful to the principles of the communist International. We swear, Comrade Lenin, to dedicate our lives to strengthening and increasing the links between the workers of the whole world in the communist International.

> *The procession returns to the back in a semi-circle and goes off.*
> LEV SEDOV *enters. He goes to* TROTSKY.

LEV SEDOV. Father. A telephone call from Berlin. Zina is dead. She locked herself in her room. Turned on the gas.

> TROTSKY *sits in a sunken attitude.* LEV SEDOV *goes off.*

12. WORLD REVOLUTION

> TROTSKY *feels his own pulse, counting softly. He shivers.* NATALIA *comes in with a rug and a newspaper. She spreads the rug over his knees and places the newspaper beside him.* TROTSKY *takes up the telescope and looks through it, describing a semi-circle towards the front.*

TROTSKY. What weather for May. Cold, damp. Grenoble shrouded in mist. But the mountain tops are clear. Can see every crack in the rocks. Like walls. The reckoning's not far off now.

NATALIA. Lyova writes from Paris. He can't find out anything about Seryosha. Our appeal has had no effect, of course. Not even the signatures of Shaw and Romain Rolland helped.

TROTSKY. The boy could bear it if he'd been active politically. Then he'd know why. But they're simply taking their revenge on him to punish me. What can they squeeze out of him? Get him to renounce me? To accuse me publicly? If only he would. If it got him back his freedom. Like Rakovsky. Rakovsky. How they must have mauled and tortured him, to make him give in. (*He opens the newspaper.*) Silver jubilee celebrations in London. The bourgeoisie putting on yet another royal show for the proletariat. There they stand, hundreds of thousands of them, lapping up all this medieval pomp and circumstance. In nineteen thirty-five. In enlightened England. I once saw it happen myself. (*He shivers again.*) How much time have we still got?

NATALIA. You're only fifty-five.

TROTSKY. Lenin said the greatest crime of all was to live past the age of fifty-five. Well, he was no criminal.

Voices are heard outside. Then a few inexpertly sung bars of the 'Internationale'. TROTSKY is startled.

They've followed us even here. (*He jumps up and takes cover behind the desk.*) They'll shoot.

NATALIA. I think it's just the students from Paris. They asked to see you.

NATALIA goes off. TROTSKY creeps beneath the desk. A group of students enters. TROTSKY takes some papers from his pocket, scatters them around and then picks them up. He rises, wipes his forehead with a hand and puts the papers on the desk.

TROTSKY. The draught.

He sits down at the desk. The students bring up chairs. The conversation begins at once.

FRENCH STUDENT. Since you're not allowed to come to Paris, we've come as a delegation to you.

GERMAN STUDENT. We have a lot of questions. Plenty to discuss. I am a German by birth. With a Jewish stamp in my passport. My father's in Dachau. Once you were against Jewish separatism. Are you still? For years German workers have been taught the virtues of international solidarity. Now they're helping to persecute Jewish families. What good is it to us that we see ourselves as Germans, not Jews? We're now labelled a different race. In the Soviet Union too

Jews are discriminated against. Couldn't the creation of a Jewish state have solved the problem?

TROTSKY. Assimilation failed as a policy. Not because the Jews themselves were against it. Rather because the Jews were still needed as a scapegoat, to divert attention from the class struggle. In Germany the pattern is shamefully clear. In the Soviet Union anti-Semitism is more difficult to pin down. When Jews are arrested, it looks as if they are being punished for criticizing the party leadership – not for being Jews.

FRENCH STUDENT. When emotions overcome dialectics, you immediately get violence and recrimination. And that leads to increased Zionism.

TROTSKY. A step backwards. I see emigration to Palestine also as a dangerous move. It can only lead to increased Arab resistance. The only solution is to fight harder to restore the International.

GERMAN STUDENT. While hundreds of thousands of Jews in Germany are going around in fear of their lives. Only Jews with money can find refuge in capitalist countries. The ones left behind, must they just accept their fate? We know the Nazis plan systematically to exterminate them.

TROTSKY. The Jews are not the only people in the world engaged in a life-and-death struggle. It is true they're paying a terrible price for their own blindness. They have done their share in helping the rise of fascism. But what is going on elsewhere? The Italians preparing to invade Ethiopia. The Japanese planning a new assault on China. The United States sending troops to Bolivia and Paraguay to safeguard their tin, their oil. Revolts in the Rhodesian copper mines brutally put down by the colonial power. Strikers in Spain shot dead. In the great world confrontation the Jews' fight for survival is of minor significance. They are merely the victims of an internal capitalist quarrel. Can't understand that overnight they've joined the ranks of the exploited.

They don't know their way about there, and won't have time
to organize their defences. That is their tragedy. The main
front is drawn between the exploited and the property-
owners. Even now, when the property-owning powers are
once again preparing to fight each other. We must keep our
sense of perspective.

FRENCH FEMALE STUDENT. You demanded a united front
with Germany. The Comintern prevented it, and fascism
conquered. In France workers of different political views
joined together spontaneously to proclaim a general strike.
The students and intellectuals supported them. But now
you, Comrade Trotsky, oppose the Popular Front government in France.

TROTSKY. A popular front is not a united front. What we want
is a common effort of workers everywhere, not an alliance
with bourgeois parties. The workers must take up arms. Set
up their own committees, their militia. Take over the
factories. All the French Popular Front does is to dissipate
the workers' energies and hold up the socialist revolution.

FRENCH FEMALE STUDENT. Why do you say we should join
up with Leon Blum's party, which isn't a revolutionary
party?

TROTSKY. To fight against reformism in its own stronghold.

FRENCH STUDENT. The most they will do is simply play us off
against the communists. We're only a tiny group. By joining
up with strange parties we destroy our own. That's no way
to set up the Fourth International.

GERMAN STUDENT. Will there ever be a Fourth International
anyway? The slump in America and England didn't produce the revolutionary situation you said it would. You
declared that the capitalist system was on the verge of collapse. At long last. How many times have you said that
already?

TROTSKY. The capitalist system stinks of corruption. The conditions are ripe for proletarian revolution. Have been for

years. The masses are on the road. But their own conserva-
tive bureaucratic machinery is holding them back. It's not
the workers who are incapable, but their leaders who are
paralysed. That's why we need a new International. Agitation, mass strikes, ultimatums, and the rotten capitalist
system would crumble.

INDO-CHINESE STUDENT. Our Indo-Chinese party will find
the way to revolution. For us the true International is the one
you and Lenin conceived. It points the way to permanent
world revolution.

TROTSKY. Don't be deceived by the smallness of our numbers.
It's not clear at the moment where revolutionary strength
really lies. My feeling, comrades, is that we can reckon with
no immediate successes in our metropolitan centres. The
coming imperialist war will perhaps destroy us all. But the
basic situation stays unchanged. The peoples at whose cost
the war is being waged will fight for their freedom. Look at
China. There a new sort of revolutionary movement has
already begun. Mao Tse-Tung is building up his army of
peasants deep in the interior. And while Chiang Kai-Shek
wages his bourgeois nationalistic battle against them, Mao
is busy forming soviets of peasants and sharing out the land.

FRENCH FEMALE STUDENT. But that contradicts your theory
that the struggle must be led by city workers.

TROTSKY. The fight began in the cities. But the revolutionary
workers were forced by the communist International to submit to the Kuomintang. You know what happened. Chiang
Kai-Shek had them butchered.

FRENCH FEMALE STUDENT. Why did the Comintern stick to
its alliance with Chiang Kai-Shek?

FRENCH STUDENT. Even made him an honorary member.

TROTSKY. Because Moscow wanted to keep the revolution
from spreading. Nothing must be allowed to interfere with
its own efforts of consolidation. In the Soviet view the revolution in China was only a bourgeois democratic revolution.

The first objective was to support China in its struggle against imperialism – England, America, Japan. That intervention switched the centre of the revolution from the towns to the country. But no one believed there was any revolutionary fervour among the peasants.

INDO-CHINESE STUDENT. You yourself once called the peasants the pack-horses of civilization. You too thought it impossible that the country people could ever form a communist party.

TROTSKY. I was afraid that Mao Tse-Tung's revolution was to much concerned with the interests of the peasants, and was losing sight of the workers. That a revolution which came to the towns from the country would lead to violent clashes with the industrial proletariat. The revolution can succeed only when the workers fight together with the peasants.

GERMAN STUDENT. For that view the Comintern demanded your head.

INDO-CHINESE STUDENT. For us the Chinese revolution provides the model. In Viet Nam there is little difference between workers, peasants, students. We all possess nothing. The word proletariat has a wider meaning for us than for you in Europe. Our first cadres and soviets were formed in the villages and plantations as well as in the factories and harbours. In order to quell the revolts the French directed their air attacks against the peasants. The colonists know that in our country the enemy is everywhere.

FRENCH STUDENT. The things that are happening in Viet Nam, in China, are in line with the theories of permanent revolution. They skip the bourgeois democratic phase. Surprise guerrilla actions all the time. Yet still both Mao Tse-Tung and the Indo-Chinese party stick outwardly to directives which are wrong for the revolution in Asia.

GERMAN STUDENT. Proof of Moscow's great reputation as the centre of world revolution.

INDO-CHINESE STUDENT. And the great influence of Lenin's

writings. Nguyen Ai Quoc, the leader of our party, has told us how he broke into tears when he first read Lenin's essays on the national and colonial problem. That was when he was an emigrant in Paris after the war. Yes, that's what we need, he cried. National heroes, martyrs. That is our way to freedom.

TROTSKY. The fight for freedom always begins where the position is most intolerable. In the darkest, most completely forgotten places.

GERMAN STUDENT. Comrade Trotsky. You have got rid of the old regime. You have fundamentally changed the whole concept of ownership. But you have not succeeded in spreading the revolution to the hearts of men.

TROTSKY. Can we transform human thinking in the space of a few years? You forget we stood alone. That the struggle for a new economic policy took all our strength.

GERMAN STUDENT. You got trapped in your own authoritarian thinking. You abolished class distinctions, yes. But you prevented the liberation of human consciousness. You, Comrade Trotsky, introduced forced labour, which is now a reality. You helped to break the power of the trade unions, leaving them helpless, as they are today. You yourself wanted complete state control over the proletariat. You ordered workers who resisted you to be shot.

TROTSKY *jumps up angrily.*

TROTSKY. The revolution was in danger of collapsing. There was no other way. You want to remove all authority, all restrictions right away. Like our old anarchists. They thought, when everything was smashed, the new order would create itself. But you forget that revolution is the most authoritarian thing on earth. One part of the population using extreme violence to enforce its will on the other part. And if the victorious part wishes to keep its power, it cannot for a long time afford to give up its weapons.

GERMAN STUDENT. Our fathers saw the October Revolution as the great beginning. But we see its weak points. What has happened to all those famous cooks?

FRENCH FEMALE STUDENT. What cooks?

GERMAN STUDENT. Lenin said any cook would be capable of running the state. Yet the workers are led by state managers. And what happened to the plans for abolishing the family, that most reactionary of institutions? It's now back to the domestic hearth, the sacred cell, the joys of motherhood. Instead of independence through learning and knowledge, you now have obedience through discipline. Instead of revolutionary art, art as the joy of new discovery, you've got sentimentality, empty idealism, fear of the unknown. Where is this new socialist man, free of selfishness, ambition, competitive instincts and base designs?

TROTSKY. I too have often had to fight hard against these nostalgic visions, comrade. Against this personal sense of the shortness of life, the vanity of effort. But then I see them before my eyes. Workers, soldiers, sailors, peasants. Men, women, old and young activists. Their faces. Their upright bodies. When I consider the mistakes of socialism, my own deficiencies, these people living today give me a clear answer. Their social system, for all its deformities, represents the greatest advance that men have ever made. In the struggle against fascism it is they who will have to carry the main load. You must support them.

AFRO-AMERICAN STUDENT. Lenin spoke in the Comintern about the black American's right to self-determination. But he didn't say how it was to be got. How can we achieve social, political and economic equality? Many of us are demanding a separate black state.

TROTSKY. That is a racialist slogan. Fight for equal rights by all means, but don't let it lead you away from the class struggle. There is a black bourgeoisie too, which shares your wish for equal rights. But ideologically it won't go further than the white workers. You are out for more. In the American class war your proletariat is the most important force, the one that will prove decisive.

AFRO-AMERICAN STUDENT. We can't join with the white workers. There's nobody more chauvinistic than they are. And they'll go on trying to keep us out of their jobs, their unions and their houses.

TROTSKY. If the white workers go on letting themselves be exploited, if they continue to believe the state is theirs just because their trade union aristocrats make deals with industry and the armed forces, then your first move must be to fight for your own liberation. That would be a huge step forward. Sign of a great moral and political awakening. And as you improve your education, a Marxist leadership is bound to arise. But you must never cut yourself off from the white proletariat. You need allies, you need a common militant party. You will be the vanguard. Remain divided, and they will finish you off one after the other.

SOUTH AMERICAN STUDENT. The American manoeuvres in Pearl Harbor, with all those huge air squadrons, the build-up of armaments, they're not only hints of what solutions are being planned for Western Europe. They also show us what we can expect in South America. Roosevelt goes on talking about good neighbourly relations. But we know it's not only the compradors we shall have to fight, but the whole might of North America. Our future lies in guerrilla warfare.

TROTSKY. The conditions in South America are different from those in China. And different again from Africa, India. In the course of whole centuries your rural population has grown used to its weakness and poverty. In China the revolutionary leaders live among the peasants. In your countries there is no common cultural background. The small farmers, the shepherds, the Indians, when you go among them, they look on you with suspicion. You don't speak their language. You grew up in the cities. Can read and write. They know nothing except their mountains, their valleys, their forests.

SOUTH AMERICAN STUDENT. Yet it is easier for us there, out in the deserts, than in the cities and industrial centres. Just because of their constant daily need, they've never learnt how to toe the line in order to gain some imagined advantage. Money has never corrupted them, since they scarcely know what money is. From them we can expect everything. They have nothing to lose.

TROTSKY. Yet I still believe it's the workers in industry, in the cities, who first realize their position. Who are willing to find out. Without a political conception, without a party, nothing can be done.

SOUTH AMERICAN STUDENT. I don't think the city parties' directives will be of much help to us, Comrade Trotsky. None of the existing theories fit our problem. Perhaps we shall have to start right at the beginning. As you did, with a handful of professional revolutionaries. Discover our strategy as we go along.

TROTSKY. Yes, I don't suggest the backward countries should simply wait patiently until the proletariat from the metropolitan centres come to free them. Conditions for armed rebellion must be created everywhere. In different ways. In the towns through political argument, through legal, semi-legal and illegal activities. In the country districts through education in its simplest form. Since the workers form a single class, they can join in pressing common demands. Through strikes, demonstrations. The illiterate small farmers are not a class. Nationalities, tribal customs, religions, superstititions, divide them. They can rise up spontaneously against profiteers, feudal landlords. Hunger, misery impels them. But to sustain a lasting revolution, you need a political conviction. That's why a rebellion, if it is to become a liberation movement, must be led by enlightened workers.

SOUTH AMERICAN STUDENT. Time will show whether objec-

tive conditions in the classical sense are necessary in Guate-
mala, Bolivia, Peru. Or whether they can't be created
through subjective surprise actions.

The students rise and prepare to leave.

FRENCH STUDENT. You know, I suppose, that down there in
the community centre, in Grenoble, Thorez and Ilya
Ehrenburg are being feted by the town. We went to the
meeting. Ehrenburg started off with a panegyric for his
government, then said hopes for preserving peace now lie in
the Red Army. In the discussion afterwards we asked him if
he was going to visit the founder of the Red Army up here in
the mountains.

The students go off laughing. TROTSKY *comes forward, takes
up the telescope and looks through it.*

13. ENEMY OF THE PEOPLE

TROTSKY *sits down. Continues to look through the telescope.*
NATALIA *comes in.*

NATALIA. Here's nothing to see but the barn and the fence.
Why don't you turn your chair round? The fjord's over
there.

TROTSKY *gets up.* NATALIA *helps him turn the chair side-
ways. He sits down again.*

TROTSKY. Can you tell the difference between a lovely view
and a less lovely one? (*Looking through the telescope.*) There's
the village down there. What's its name? I always forget.

NATALIA. Hönnefoss.

TROTSKY. You know, a little while ago I had great difficulty in
finding out exactly where I was. Nothing but empty space.
Yes. Hönnefoss. Yes. Norway. Down there on the road,
there's a car coming.

NATALIA. That will be the doctor.

TROTSKY. Was the radio mechanic here? Has he fixed the aerial?

NATALIA. Yes. We can hear Moscow now.

A doctor comes in with an assistant. The doctor goes straight to TROTSKY. *The assistant strolls about, looking around in a searching way, eyeing the papers on the desk.*

TROTSKY. Difficulty in breathing. Pressure here on the chest. Pulse irregular, sometimes racing. Giddiness. Loss of memory. Yes, complete loss of memory.

DOCTOR. Take off your shirt.

TROTSKY *takes off his jacket and shirt. The doctor goes over him with a stethoscope, sounds his chest.*

Take a deep breath. Cough.

TROTSKY *coughs laboriously.*

Lungs and heart in order. Thorax remarkably strong.

TROTSKY. But in the night. I can't sleep. Lie bathed in sweat.

DOCTOR. Nervous strain. Quite understandable. Yes, quite understandable. (*He laughs heartily.*)

TROTSKY. Why are you laughing?

DOCTOR. You know Ibsen? An enemy of the people. You're Doctor Stockmann, to the life. The lone wolf. The man who won't conform to the general pattern, won't submit.

TROTSKY. So far as I remember, Stockmann unmasked the corruption in his town.

DOCTOR. Even if he was right in certain things, he was the loser in the end. He hadn't the talent of passing on his knowledge. He despised the crowd, the masses, that cursed compact majority. He was the intellectual aristocrat. A helpless, really rather tragic figure. The way he whines out his credo at the end: strongest is he who stands alone.

The doctor laughs again. TROTSKY *jumps up.*

TROTSKY. Who are you?

The doctor laughs. TROTSKY *turns to his assistant.*

And you? What are you looking for? Why are you prying about among my things?

The doctor and assistant go off laughing. NATALIA *comes in.*

We must ask Knudsen for a guard. People can come and go here as they like. Who was that? Not a doctor.

In the background the prosecutor in the Moscow trials appears. His words are occasionally indistinct, cut off.

PROSECUTOR. Preliminary investigations have revealed that all the accused carried on their despicable traitorous activities on the instructions of Trotsky, that enemy of the people who now lives abroad. Proof will be brought to show that through the efforts of this counter-revolutionary Trotskyist rabble the lives of our most prominent party leaders and government officials were – (*Sound interrupted.*) Their aim was to undermine our economic and military strength, to encourage an armed attack by the fascists, to help foreign aggressors seize and share out our territory, to bring about the downfall of Soviet power and restore a capitalist regime – (*Sound interrupted.*) These accursed parasites, deviationists, spies and terrorists, this miserable band of swindlers and murderers – (*Sound interrupted.*) The accused: Zinoviev, Kamenev, Smirnov, Rykov, Mrachkovsky, Pyatakov, Radek, Bukharin, Rakovsky, Antonov, Shlyapnikov, Tukhachevsky –

Enter ZINOVIEV, KAMENEV, SMIRNOV, MRACHKOVSKY, PYATAKOV, RADEK, BUKHARIN, RAKOVSKY *and the witness* ZAFONOVA. *They position themselves at widely spaced intervals.* NATALIA *is seated at back.* TROTSKY *stands at front, with bare chest, his shirt in his hand.*

Defendant Mrachkovsky. You were Trotsky's closest

confidant. You have worked with him against the Soviet
Union since nineteen twenty-three. Were a member of the
committee in the illegal Trotskyist organization –

MRACHKOVSKY. When I returned from banishment in nineteen twenty-nine I signed a statement supporting the
general party line. But in fact I came back as a double agent,
to continue the fight against the party. In nineteen thirty-one
our group openly discussed the question of terrorism.
Smirnov brought a directive from Trotsky, which he had
been given by Trotsky's son Sedov in Berlin.

PROSECUTOR. What did this directive say?

MRACHKOVSKY. Until the party leaders were set aside, we
could not come to power.

PROSECUTOR. What was meant by set aside?

MRACHKOVSKY. It meant murdered. But the Trotskyist group
was too weak by itself, so it became a question of working
together with other counter-revolutionary groups. Trotsky
was in favour of joining up with the Zinoviev people, but he
said the block must be built up on the basis of terrorism.

PROSECUTOR. Defendant Zinoviev. When was this joint
organization formed?

ZINOVIEV. In the summer of thirty-two.

PROSECUTOR. And what did it plan to do?

ZINOVIEV. The most important thing was to prepare terrorist
acts.

PROSECUTOR. Against whom?

ZINOVIEV. Against the top leaders of the party.

PROSECUTOR. Defendant Smirnov. Did you receive this
directive about the use of terror from Trotsky?

SMIRNOV *is silent.*

Defendant Mrachkovsky. You met Smirnov after his return
from Berlin?

MRACHKOVSKY. Yes.

PROSECUTOR. You spoke with him?

MRACHKOVSKY. Yes.

PROSECUTOR. Together with Zafonova?

MRACHKOVSKY. Yes.

PROSECUTOR. Smirnov brought you Trotsky's instructions?

MRACHKOVSKY. Yes.

PROSECUTOR. Smirnov, did you hear that?

SMIRNOV *is silent.*

Defendant Zinoviev. Was terrorism the basis on which your group joined forces with the Trotskyists?

ZINOVIEV. Yes. We were convinced that the leaders must be removed at all costs. That we must remove them together with Trotsky.

PROSECUTOR. Defendant Zinoviev. Both you and Kamenev followed two different courses simultaneously. You did all you could to demonstrate your loyalty to the party. At the same time you were personally preparing acts of terror against the party leaders. Do you plead guilty to this heinous crime?

ZINOVIEV. Yes.

PROSECUTOR. I ask the defendant Kamenev the same question.

KAMENEV. My answer is affirmative.

PROSECUTOR. Defendant Kamenev. How are we to interpret the statements you made in nineteen thirty-three, proclaiming your loyalty to the party? Was this deceit?

KAMENEV. Worse than deceit.

PROSECUTOR. Perfidy?

KAMENEV. Worse than perfidy.

PROSECUTOR. Worse than deceit. Worse than perfidy. Find the word for it. Treason.

KAMENEV. You have found it.

PROSECUTOR. What were your reasons?

KAMENEV. We had lost all hope of splitting the party leadership. That left us with two alternatives. Either to abandon

our resistance completely, or to pursue it – without hope of
any mass support of any kind, without a political platform
or an ideology – simply through individual acts of terror.
We chose the second course. We gave in to our feelings of
bitterness against the party leaders and to our greed for
power.

PROSECUTOR. Your fight against the party leadership and the
government was based on vile motives of personal lust for
power?

KAMENEV. Yes. On the group's lust for power.

PROSECUTOR. Had that anything to do with social ideals?

KAMENEV. It had only to do with the things that revolution
and counter-revolution have in common.

PROSECUTOR. So you stand on the side of counter-revolution?

KAMENEV. Yes.

PROSECUTOR. It was a deliberate attack on socialism?

KAMENEV. It was a deliberate attack on the party and
government which are leading the country towards
socialism.

PROSECUTOR. Which means you are also against socialism?

KAMENEV. You draw the conclusion of a historian and a
prosecutor.

PROSECUTOR. Defendant Smirnov. You are a close friend of
Trotsky's. You are named as the leader of the Trotskyist
centre. You conveyed Trotsky's instructions on the use of
terrorism to your illegal organization.

SMIRNOV. I did not think this information was to be inter-
preted as a definite instruction by Trotsky.

PROSECUTOR. Defendant Mrachkovsky. What was contained
in Trotsky's directive?

MRACHKOVSKY. It said there was nothing more to be got from
our previous methods of fighting. We must turn to other, to
sharper methods. It said it was childish to think bureaucracy
could be overcome by a revolution in the Soviet Congress.
Normal procedures were no longer enough to bring down

the leaders of the party and the government. Only force could get them out.

TROTSKY *jumps up.*

TROTSKY. Yes, revolutionary force. That's what I wrote. And not in a secret directive, but in an open letter. I said power must be transferred to the *avant-garde* of the proletariat. Anyone can read it. A demand for a return to revolutionary tradition, which you are distorting into a conspiracy of individual terror.

PROSECUTOR. Defendant Smirnov. Was the centre organized on the basis of terror?

SMIRNOV *is silent.*

What do you admit?

SMIRNOV. I admit I was implicated in the illegal Trotskyist organization, that I joined the block, that I joined the centre of this block, that I saw Sedov in Berlin in nineteen thirty-one and listened to his views on terrorism, which I then, without agreeing with them, conveyed to Moscow.

PROSECUTOR. Witness Zafonova. Did Smirnov in your presence speak of the need to commit terrorist acts against the party leaders?

ZAFONOVA. He spoke of Trotsky's instruction that the centre should start to use terrorist methods.

PROSECUTOR. Did he speak of the need to murder the party leaders?

ZAFONOVA. He said categorically the party leaders must be killed.

PROSECUTOR. Defendant Smirnov. What were your relations with Zafonova?

SMIRNOV. Friendly.

PROSECUTOR. Nothing more?

SMIRNOV. We were very close.

PROSECUTOR. You were man and wife?

SMIRNOV. Yes.

PROSECUTOR. There are no personal differences between you?

SMIRNOV. No.

PROSECUTOR. Defendant Smirnov. You admit the block adopted the standpoint of terrorism?

SMIRNOV. Yes.

PROSECUTOR. You admit the block adopted this standpoint in connection with Trotsky's directives?

SMIRNOV. Yes.

PROSECUTOR. And it was you who received the directives?

SMIRNOV. Yes.

PROSECUTOR. And who passed them on to the block?

SMIRNOV. Yes.

PROSECUTOR. So consequently it was you who brought the block to the standpoint of terrorism.

SMIRNOV *is silent.*

Defendant Smirnov. The circle is completed.

SMIRNOV *sinks to his knees, then collapses. Two soldiers, bayonets fixed to their slung rifles, go quickly to* SMIRNOV *and drag him off.* ZAFONOVA *follows them.*

Defendant Pyatakov. What have you to say about your criminal Trotskyist activities against the Soviet Union?

PYATAKOV. I received orders from Trotsky to obstruct all government measures, particularly in the field of economics.

PROSECUTOR. Where were you working at that time?

PYATAKOV. In the Supreme Economic Council, as chairman for the chemical industry.

PROSECUTOR. And while enjoying the government's confidence, you were busy going around sabotaging and spying against the Soviet state?

PYATAKOV. Our criminal activities led to catastrophes in the coalmines, motor factories, steel works, shipbuilding yards and power plants. We disrupted traffic, slowed down the building of houses and impeded agricultural production. We also carried out mass poisonings of Soviet workers.

PROSECUTOR. Was all this done on your own initiative or on instructions from others?

PYATAKOV. Mostly according to directives from Trotsky.

PROSECUTOR. What was Trotsky trying to achieve?

PYATAKOV. Trotsky wrote there was nothing accidental about his policy of destruction. It wasn't just one of the sharper forms of fighting he had been recommending, but a very important part of his whole plan. He said – that was in nineteen thirty-four – that Hitler's victory had clearly shown he was right in arguing that socialism could not be built up in one single country. He said war was inevitable, and we Trotskyists, if we wanted to stay alive as a political force, must actively plot the downfall of the Soviet Union.

PROSECUTOR. You were working for a Soviet military defeat?

PYATAKOV. That was the goal. Since in Trotsky's view the war would be first with Germany and then possibly with Japan, our task was to reach an understanding with the governments of these countries and win their support for the block's attempt to assume power. A number of concessions were to be agreed with these countries in advance, so they would help the block remain in power. Radek received detailed instructions in a letter at the end of nineteen thirty-five.

PROSECUTOR. Defendant Radek, did you receive such a letter or letters?

RADEK. I received a letter in April thirty-four and a second in December thirty-five. In the first Trotsky said the war would lead to a Soviet defeat. This defeat would enable the block to assume power. For this reason the block must try to hasten the outbreak of war and thus ensure the downfall of the Soviet Union.

PROSECUTOR. And what had the second letter to say?

RADEK. In effect it amounted to a return to capitalism. Restoration of a capitalist system. As a result of the defeat, he foresaw that important industrial rights would be ceded to Germany and Japan. In production generally the private sector would regain an effective interest. And finally the collective farms would be handed over to a new class of kulaks.

PROSECUTOR. Did Trotsky speak of territorial concessions?

RADEK. He indicated that territorial concessions would be necessary.

PROSECUTOR. What sort of concessions?

RADEK. If we wanted friendship with the Germans, he wrote, we should have to do something to recognize and satisfy their need for expansion.

PROSECUTOR. Surrender the Ukraine?

RADEK. We were in no doubt the Ukraine was meant. Regarding Japan, Trotsky spoke of giving up the Far Eastern coast areas.

PROSECUTOR. Had Trotsky already started negotiations with the German and Japanese governments?

RADEK. He was in touch with Hess, Hitler's deputy. He had told representatives of the Japanese government he would put no obstacles in the way of Japan's conquest of China.

PROSECUTOR. Defendant Pyatakov. Do you confirm that this is what the letters said?

PYATAKOV. Yes, I confirm it.

TROTSKY. Natasha, why doesn't Lyova send the documents? What is he doing in Paris – just sitting about? Every single point can be refuted. But we must be quick. Or they'll all be destroyed.

PROSECUTOR. Did you never find it necessary to speak personally with Trotsky?

PYATAKOV. A meeting in Norway was arranged. I agreed to go, though it was very dangerous for me.

PROSECUTOR. Where were you at that time?

PYATAKOV. At the beginning of December nineteen thirty-five I was in Berlin on official business. On the twelfth of December, early in the morning, I flew from the Tempelhof airport and landed at three in the afternoon on an airfield near Oslo. A car was waiting for me. We drove about thirty minutes and came to a residential suburb. We got out and went into a small house, quite well furnished. And there I met Trotsky, whom I hadn't seen since nineteen twenty-eight.

TROTSKY. Did you have a Norwegian visa? Could you leave Berlin without telling the Soviet Embassy where you were going? How did you manage to keep out of sight of the Soviet people in Oslo? What plane did you use?

PROSECUTOR. Defendant Pyatakov. You landed on a Norwegian airfield?

PYATAKOV. Yes. Near Oslo.

PROSECUTOR. What was the name of the airfield?

PYATAKOV. I don't know its name.

PROSECUTOR. Were there any difficulties on landing?

PYATAKOV. No. I drove immediately to the suburb where Trotsky was expecting me.

TROTSKY. I live two hours away from Oslo, not thirty minutes, and in the mountains.

PROSECUTOR. Was anyone else present at your meeting?

PYATAKOV. Nobody at all. The whole meeting took place in complete secrecy.

TROTSKY. Didn't you see my wife? Did we offer you nothing to eat? You must have been hungry after your long journey.

PROSECUTOR. What did you talk about?

PYATAKOV. I told him what the centre had been doing so far. He kept interrupting me. Making sarcastic remarks about appeasement, failure to appreciate the situation. Said we were living in a fool's paradise. Still tied by the navel to the party. He said many of us Trotskyists were still labouring under the delusion that a mass rising could be organized. This was

impossible, he told me, because the workers and the farming
population were hypnotized by the social recovery programme, which they still imagined to be a socialist programme. He said we could only come to power through a
coup d'état, with all that meant in terms of fighting methods.

PROSECUTOR. Did he speak of his negotiations with the
deputy leader of the German National Socialist Party?

PYATAKOV. He told me he'd come to an agreement with Hess
that German capital would be used in the Soviet Union to
exploit the supply of raw materials.

PROSECUTOR. Was there anything new in Trotsky's instructions?

PYATAKOV. What was new was made very clear. The Trotskyist organization was being turned into a tool of fascism.

   NATALIA *comes forward.*

NATALIA. Knudsen confirms that in the winter of thirty-five no
foreign or private plane from Berlin landed on the Kjeller
airfield near Oslo. As Trotsky's host in Norway he declares
there was no meeting of any kind there between Pyatakov
and Trotsky.

PROSECUTOR. Defendant Pyatakov. Was the airfield named
Kjeller?

PYATAKOV. Possibly it was Kjeller.

PROSECUTOR. The Soviet representatives in Oslo inform us
that Kjeller is open to air traffic from all countries the whole
year through.

PYATAKOV. Citizen judges. In this moment in which we have
to assume before Soviet justice the full responsibility for our
crimes, the man in whose name and at whose instigation we
committed them will find no other way out than to deny all
the things we did together with him, slander us, lie and accuse us of giving false evidence.

PROSECUTOR. Defendant Rakovsky. You were Trotsky's
personal friend?

RAKOVSKY. I was his personal friend.

PROSECUTOR. You shared his political views?

RAKOVSKY. I shared his political views.

PROSECUTOR. Why did you wage this battle against the Soviet state?

RAKOVSKY. We acted in a state of delirium. The important and responsible positions we occupied in the state turned our heads. In our self-delusion we did not stop short of deceit, corruption, murder, to win power for ourselves. And so in the end we formed alliances with Hitler and the Japanese emperor, in order to destroy the achievements of the socialist recovery programme in the Soviet Union and restore capitalist conditions. Our revolutionary habits turned into counter-revolutionary habits.

PROSECUTOR. What revolutionary habits had you got?

RAKOVSKY. One cannot deny that I once belonged –

PROSECUTOR. You never belonged among the revolutionaries. You fascist hireling.

RAKOVSKY. Yes, I am guilty of high treason. As early as nineteen twenty-four I became a member of the British intelligence service. On my release from exile in nineteen thirty-four I became an agent of the Japanese secret service. But when we thought we could seize power and keep it without handing it over to the fascists, that was madness, Utopia. Citizen judges, I do not want to transfer my guilt to Trotsky. I am older than he. Have no less political experience. But I regret that he, Trotsky, the enemy of the people, is not here being charged along with us. I regret it, because this trial loses something of its breadth and depth when he, the leader of the conspiracy, is lacking. I regret it, because Trotsky's absence means he can continue his activities. But I am certain, even in his Mexican hide-out, to which he has now crept following his expulsion from Norway, I am confident he will not escape the dishonour we are suffering here.

RADEK. I cannot even claim that Trotsky led me astray. I went along with the Trotskyist organization not on account of his pitiable theories, which I knew to be rotten ever since I first heard them during my first exile, but because there was no other group on which I could have relied to achieve my own political aims. I have admitted my treachery. But what proofs are there for the crimes we committed? How can you know for certain that the things we have said are the whole truth and nothing but the truth? There is my statement that I received letters and directives from Trotsky, which I have unfortunately burnt. There is Pyatakov's statement concerning his meeting with Trotsky. All the statements made by the other defendants rest on our confessions. Comrade judges –

PROSECUTOR. Not comrade, defendant Radek. Citizen judges.

RADEK. I beg your pardon. Citizen judges. Though I am not entitled to put myself forward as a repentant communist, I may still say that we have spent the main part of our lives in the workers' movement, and that the masses, with whom we once marched together, still mean something to us. Before these, believe me, we are not lying now. We say to everyone who is fighting in the interests of peace, we say to the whole world, Trotskyism is the tool of fascists and warmongers. It's very hard for us to admit this. But it's a historical fact. A fact for which we shall pay with our heads.

MRACHKOVSKY. I am a worker. Son and grandson of working men. Son and grandchild –

PROSECUTOR. You are a traitor to the working class, Mrachkovsky. A traitor to the revolution.

MRACHKOVSKY. I was arrested for the first time when I was thirteen. Let everyone remember that workers too, or people who have come from the working class like me, can turn into counter-revolutionaries. I do not deserve to live any longer. But I beg you to believe me when I say I have now washed away all the dirt I covered myself with.

ZINOVIEV. Against the party none of us can be in the right.

At the last reckoning the party is always right, because it is the only historical instrument the working classes have to fulfil their purposes. After Lenin's death it was I who urged Trotsky to accept this fundamental principle. But he refused. He broke the law. Yet in spite of that I joined up with him. My defective bolshevism turned into anti-Bolshevism. I became an enemy of the international workers' movement.

BUKHARIN. Once we stood beside Lenin –

PROSECUTOR. Hypocrite. You, Bukharin, never stood beside Lenin.

BUKHARIN. Then we tried to destroy Lenin's work, which is today being continued with such gigantic success by the present party leaders. But we ourselves have been destroyed. The Trotskyist conspiracy is smashed to pieces. I go down on my knees before the party, before the whole people, before the wise leaders of our country.

> SMIRNOV *is led in by armed soldiers. He stands bowed and speaks tonelessly.*

SMIRNOV. I speak to the scattered remnants of Trotskyists who still roam the country, to all who have not yet ceased to resist. I say to them: lay down your arms. Turn your backs on Trotsky and Trotskyism. There is no other path for our country but the one it is now treading. It can have no other leadership than that which history has given us.

> *At back appear a number of nameless prisoners, accompanied by soldiers. Some of them come forward.*

PROSECUTOR. I demand that these mad dogs should all be shot. Weeds and thistles shall cover their graves. They shall be despised for ever by upright Soviet men, by the whole Soviet people.

> *The main defendants are led by soldiers to the back.* ZINOVIEV *resists.*

ZINOVIEV. You promised us our lives if we confessed.

Laughter among the soldiers. ZINOVIEV *clutches one soldier round the legs.*

Please, for the love of heaven. Call Iosif Vissarionovich. He promised us personally.

KAMENEV. I speak to my children. Do not look back. Go forward. Together with the Soviet people.

SMIRNOV. Free my wife, my daughter.

ZINOVIEV *is dragged off. He screams.*

ZINOVIEV. Hear, O Israel. Hear, O Israel. Our god is the one god.

While the group is being led off, some of the nameless prisoners go to TROTSKY.

FIRST PRISONER. They didn't dare bring Shlyapnikov into court. He'd have spat in the prosecutor's face. They finished him off in the cellars, along with thousands of others who wouldn't confess. Peterson was among them. The soldier from Latvia who once drove your armoured train.

SECOND PRISONER. Before they shot Antonov he gave his coat, jacket and shoes to his fellow prisoners. He asked us, if we ever got free, to tell everybody Antonov was a Bolshevik, and remained a Bolshevik to the last.

THIRD PRISONER. They took your son Sergey back to Moscow. He held out through all the interrogations and tortures. Refused to sign any declarations. They shot him through the back of the neck.

FOURTH PRISONER. Lyova is dead. Was taken to hospital in Paris. Poisoned. Wandered round the corridors, raving. You'll be the next.

All the prisoners go off. Only NATALIA *remains at the back, sunk down on a chair.* TROTSKY *stands at front, with hang-*

ing arms, shirt still in hand. He stands some moments without moving.

Suddenly the sound of machine-gun fire. NATALIA *jumps up.* TROTSKY *runs to the desk, tips it over and takes cover behind it.* NATALIA *throws herself protectively over him. More shots are heard.*

14. THE TESTAMENT

Several people enter: ROSMER, SYLVIA AGELOF, FRANK JACSON, JOSEPH HANSEN, HAROLD ROBINS, *a few Mexican policemen and* COLONEL SALAZAR, *chief of the Mexican secret police.*

TROTSKY *and* NATALIA *get to their feet.*

SALAZAR. You're not hurt?

TROTSKY *feels his body, laughs and puts on his shirt.* TROTSKY's *friends and assistants look after* NATALIA. *She is also unhurt. The desk is put upright.* ROBINS *rearranges papers, books and writing materials on the desk. The policemen search the room for bullet holes.*

JACSON. There were more than twenty of them. In police uniform. Overcame the guard. Slugged them, tied them up.

TROTSKY. How did they get in? Over the wall? Through the electric fence? Why didn't the alarm go off?

JACSON. Sheldon let them through the gate. He was with the guards.

SALAZAR. Who is this Sheldon?

JACSON. They took him with them.

SALAZAR. Do you think he was one of them?

TROTSKY. Sheldon Harte? Impossible. If he'd wanted to kill me, he wouldn't have needed twenty assistants. Only a knife.

SALAZAR. And the other people in the house?

TROTSKY. This is Sylvia Agelof, an American comrade. Frank
Jacson, her friend. This my secretary, Harold Robins. Joseph
Hansen, Alfred Rosmer, close assistants for many years.

SALAZAR. The attackers had a complete knowledge of the
territory. Took cover behind the trees in the yard. Shot into
your room from several different points.

FIRST POLICEMAN. I counted thirty-seven bullet holes in the
wall.

TROTSKY. I thought at first you Mexicans had been letting off
fireworks again.

SALAZAR. I can't understand how you can be so calm. The
attack was only possible with the help of persons close to
you. (*He takes* TROTSKY *aside.*) Anyone you suspect? The
servants?

TROTSKY. We trust them implicitly.

SALAZAR. Your secretaries?

TROTSKY. Absolutely reliable.

SALAZAR. We shall have to question them.

TROTSKY. I should object most strongly.

SALAZAR. So many attackers. So many firearms. Even bombs.
And no one was injured. Strange. Who do you think was
responsible?

TROTSKY *laughs.*

TROTSKY. I will tell you. The GPU.

A few policemen from the motor-cycle squad enter.

SECOND POLICEMAN. We've got one of the cars in which they
escaped. Arrested a few. They say their leader is Siqueiros.

TROTSKY. Siqueiros, the painter?

SECOND POLICEMAN. David Alfaro Siqueiros. The group he
got together were former members of the Spanish international brigade, and miners.

ROSMER. Siqueiros. He came out against the Trotskyists
before, in Spain.

TROTSKY. So heavy an attack. So carefully prepared. And such a miserable failure.

THIRD POLICEMAN. They say they only wanted to frighten Trotsky.

ROSMER. With real bullets. More than three hundred shots were fired.

TROTSKY. The Comintern has made a fool of itself again.

HANSEN. The doors and windows must be bullet-proofed. The watch-tower heightened. A better alarm system installed

JACSON. The next time they'll use a different method.

HANSEN. What sort of method?

> JACSON *shrugs his shoulders.* SALAZAR *and the policemen go off.*

TROTSKY. Jacson, take a look at the rabbits, will you? They must have had quite a shock.

> JACSON *and* SYLVIA AGELOF *go off.*

HANSEN. I don't trust that man Jacson. When he was in New York the other day he didn't visit our headquarters.

TROTSKY. You must be nice to him. Bring him round to our way of thinking. We must always work from the assumption that people can be changed.

NATALIA. What is Jacson actually doing?

TROTSKY. Transporting Belgian diamond cutters to Mexico.

HANSEN. You must never see people alone.

TROTSKY. We can't suspect everybody.

HANSEN. All visitors must be searched.

TROTSKY. I can't adopt these American customs. We must admit our friends without question.

HANSEN. The enemy can profess to be your friend.

TROTSKY. Then I can't hope to escape him. I can't cut myself off. Can't work in seclusion. Impossible, this constant self-protection. Takes the whole meaning out of life. We're already living in a medieval stronghold. These heavy doors. These walls. Like my first prison in Kherson.

> ROBINS *has meanwhile very meticulously restored order to the desk.* ROBINS *and* NATALIA *go off. Enter* DIEGO RIVERA *and* ANDRÉ BRETON.

RIVERA. Siqueiros. Hero of the Spanish civil war. Leader of the Mexican miners. What was he trying to do? Demonstrate the unity of revolution and art? Or just make an impression on the party?

TROTSKY. Fundamentally, Diego, he was following my argument that the Soviet Union must be protected at all costs. We all know the Soviet alliance with the German fascists is simply playing for time. Sooner or later it must come to a fight. It is a difficult situation, and a dangerous course to steer. Siqueiros, like all other loyal party followers, still sees me as the arch-enemy. Just by being alive I disturb the present leaders. Siqueiros wanted to liquidate me, on higher orders.

RIVERA. So the trials did what they set out to do. You stand condemned for all time, though we have proved the terrible slanders made against you false in every detail.

TROTSKY. Diego, imagine the word got round that Diego Rivera is a secret agent of the Catholic church. All his great frescoes, castigating the church and the world of exploiters, are camouflage, painted to conceal his real opinions. Who would believe it for long? Could you proclaim the ideas of world revolution with such passion, in the face of such persecution, if at heart you were a reactionary?

BRETON. Many could believe even that. We live in a time of insane disfigurements and distortions. The powers of forgery are so immense that the individual is helpless against them. The accused men in Moscow did not shout: it's all lies, everything we said in evidence is a lie. The whole world press was there. One word would have done to tear the whole monstrous swindle to pieces. But they themselves were already caught up in the swindle. Accepted the necessity of the whole crazy argument. So we could all together commit suicide, collectively.

TROTSKY. When things are hard to understand, Breton, that's the very time we must apply our reason. It's our only weapon. Once we say the butcherings, the self-sacrificings, were unbelievable, we've joined the side of the hangmen. We *can* show why the victims acted as they did. We *must* show it. If we don't make clear exactly what happened, the Soviet Union will perish.

BRETON. Why did they let themselves be stripped of all their honour? They, the pioneers of socialism, why did they let the others trample their faces in the mud? They were the very best. A whole generation of revolutionaries. All leading Bolsheviks. What did they prove with their surrender but the bankruptcy of their ideas?

HANSEN. They were convinced communists to the end. Their whole life devoted to the party. Their solidarity with it complete, even when they knew it was on the wrong track. Presumably they felt bound to submit to the majority decision, to do what the party demanded of them.

BRETON. That is religious mysticism. Union with the godhead. Renunciation of individual judgement. As in the Inquisition. The victims accept punishment as being good for them.

HANSEN. I can't share André Breton's view that they weren't conscious the whole trial was a lie. Some comrades explain the false statements, the bogus confessions this way: the accused men knew that in Germany and Italy the proletariat was totally defeated. There was no chance now of revolutionary help from outside. On one side Germany, on the other Japan. War was unavoidable. So the party leaders, however hateful, had to be supported. Better the absolute rule of a tyrant than uncertainty, defeatism in the face of fascist aggression. They made themselves the scapegoats for all the country's mistakes and misfortunes. Hoping in that way to put new heart into the people, once they believed the alleged trouble-makers had all been rooted out.

BRETON. Not a very rational explanation. Rather a psychiatric diagnosis. Self-humiliation of that kind has no meaning politically. It does nothing except show the wide gap between an impersonal abstract world and the most elementary of human rights. The all-powerful centralized party forced new compulsions on its citizens, instead of freeing them from such things for ever. And so destroyed the ideals from which the revolutionaries had set out. It's exactly the same with art. Independent thinking is completely wiped out. No truly revolutionary approach is possible any more. I heard Eisenstein's terrible confession of guilt. He went down on his knees and pleaded for mercy. Promised to root out the last remnants of his anarchistic individualism and seek the correct approach with the help of the party.

RIVERA. Meyerhold and Isaak Babel didn't grovel. Nor did many others. When besotted small-minded functionaries won't allow the country's best theatre director, its best writer to work, what have they left to live for?

ROSMER. One's always asking oneself: which showed the most courage? The people who stood up and faced their accusers in court, or those who refused to sign any confessions? Who chose to be finished off in dark cellars and slung into unknown pits.

BRETON. Above the claim of loyalty to the party there is a yet higher claim: the claim of truth. It's this self-betrayal, the refusal to speak out that's turning Marxism into a graveyard. There is one fact that can't be ignored: the fighters of the October Revolution let themselves be destroyed simply because they stood in the tyrant's way.

HANSEN. Breton, remember the background. Beside the urge to save the party, the prisoners faced horrors of a sort we can't imagine. All of them subjected to torture for months on end, even years. Their wives and children held as hostages. Even twelve-year-olds could be legally executed. They thought by confessing they could save their families. Don't forget the part desperation played in formulating their statements.

BRETON. Yet all the same they inflicted a wound on socialism from which it will never recover. What had they been fighting for? For humanity and consideration in politics. For an end to terroristic party power. For a broadening of democracy. And how did they present themselves at the end? As traitors and deserters, whose only aim was to restore the bourgeois society they had spent their lives in destroying. Lenin's entire Politburo nothing but a band of crooks and blackguards. What a slap in the face for the workers' movement.

TROTSKY. I agree with you, Breton, that the Russian people were deceived, both by the murderers in the party and their victims. I also agree that the social order designed to end men's fight against their fellow men has now itself become an instrument directed against human beings. But I do not agree when you say socialism can never recover from this great historical shock. What has happened shows, not that socialism is wrong, but that our revolutionary acts have exposed our weakness and inexperience. We have not succeeded in overcoming human frailty, human cowardice, human baseness. Remember, the experiment in the Soviet Union is hardly more than twenty years old. In China the revolution still goes on. In Indo-China, I hear, the liberation movement is gaining in strength. In South America unrest is increasing. In the war in Europe the workers will find themselves again. And the Soviet Union can once more show the way to revolution if it dares to admit past mistakes and betrayals and to remove their causes. Against socialism that other system still stands firm: the system of absolute baseness, absolute greed, absolute selfishness. That system cannot change. It can only, by its very nature, become more predatory, more destructive. But socialism, in spite of the crimes committed in its name, can change. It can be improved, can be given new life.

RIVERA. You've seen all the people crushed and mangled who tried to break out of the stranglehold on thought, who fought against the growing restrictions, the compulsory conformity. You have seen all your companions destroyed. And yet you are still an optimist?

TROTSKY. I can't stop believing in reason, in human solidarity. The older I get, the more strongly I believe. I have never known personal tragedy. My life has been bound up insolubly with all the successive phases of the revolution. Failures and disappointments can't stop me from seeing beyond the present defeat to a rising of the oppressed everywhere. This is no Utopian prophecy. It is the sober prediction of a dialectical materialist. I have never lost my faith in the revolutionary power of the masses. But we must be prepared for a long fight. For years, maybe decades, of revolts, civil wars, new revolts, new wars. And if sometimes it looks as if the class war is flagging, the leaders crumbling under the threats and lies of the bourgeois regime, there are always new generations to come. Students. As it was in Russia at the turn of the century. But this time in a single, all-embracing movement. From the universities of all countries and continents. They will take up the fight and drive it forward. They will find a common language, a common line of action with the progressive workers. The privations and sacrifices will be borne by the working class, but they too will shoulder the burden of reconstruction, building up again. Then victory over world capitalism will be possible, when a revolutionary party once again stands at the head of the proletariat. If death were to strike me today, I could say I had worked for the exploited and colonized masses in the permanent struggle for liberation. For the need of culture and science to develop freely. For an art that allows unrestricted expression to man's urge for renewal. For an expansion of technology which, once we understand how to use the energy of the atom, will lighten our existence. And always in my mind the dominating thought has been international revolution. This in the end can put an end to exploitation, violence and war.

All present go off. TROTSKY *goes to the desk, sits down and completes the arrangement of his writing materials and papers. He remains a few moments in the position as at the beginning.*

15. THE EXECUTION

TROTSKY *straightens up.* NATALIA *appears at front.*

TROTSKY. Beautiful. Life is beautiful. This shining grass. White walls. The blue sky behind you. It's a long time since I felt so well.

NATALIA *comes up beside him and puts a hand on his shoulder.*

You know, Natalia, on this stage you are the main character. (*They laugh.*) We have lived together nearly forty years. Forty years. Inconceivable without you.

NATALIA *kisses him on the forehead.*

NATALIA. Jacson is outside. He wants to show you his essay.
TROTSKY. Yes, on the situation in occupied France. I can't imagine it will say very much. (*He laughs.*) But we must encourage him.

JACSON *appears at front from the side. He is wearing a hat and holds a raincoat pressed against his side.* NATALIA *goes towards him.*

NATALIA. Why the hat and coat? It's so hot.

JACSON. There are thunder clouds over the mountains. It might rain.

NATALIA. I've never seen you with a coat before, even in the rain.

JACSON *gives a nervous laugh.*

You don't look well, Jacson.

JACSON. I feel a bit sick. Full up to here. (*He moves a hand jerkily to his throat.*)

NATALIA. Would you like a cup of tea?

JACSON. Water, perhaps. I've got a terrible thirst.

NATALIA *goes off.* JACSON *crosses to the desk. He clumsily extracts a manuscript from the pocket of the raincoat, holding the coat close against his body.* TROTSKY *takes the manuscript.* JACSON *sits on the edge of the desk. He is still wearing his hat.*

TROTSKY. Good, it's typewritten. Makes it easier to read.

He bends over the manuscript, as at the beginning of the play. NATALIA *comes in with a glass of water, which she gives to* JACSON. *He drinks it all.*

NATALIA. How is Sylvia?

JACSON. Sylvia? Sylvia?

NATALIA. Isn't Sylvia coming today? I thought you were leaving together.

JACSON *nods.*

Then I'll see you afterwards in the garden.

NATALIA *goes off.* TROTSKY, *bending over the manuscript, pen in hand, reads a while. Then he turns with an irritable gesture to* JACSON, *who is still sitting on the corner of the desk.* JACSON *stands up, grinning nervously. He stands behind* TROTSKY, *waiting.* TROTSKY *sits motionless over the manuscript, as at the beginning.* JACSON *silently moves up close behind him. Slowly he pulls an ice axe from the raincoat. Its handle has been shortened. With both hands he lifts the axe high over* TROTSKY'S *head and prepares to bring it down.*

BLACKOUT

Methuen's Modern Plays

EDITED BY JOHN CULLEN

Methuen's Theatre Classics

Methuen Playscripts

Paul Ableman	*Tests*
	Blue Comedy
Barry Bermange	*Nathan and Tabileth* and *Oldenberg*
John Bowen	*The Corsican Brothers*
Howard Brenton	*Revenge*
	Christie in Love and other plays
Henry Chapman	*You Won't Always be on Top*
Peter Cheeseman (Ed.)	*The Knotty*
David Cregan	*Three Men for Colverton*
	Transcending and *The Dancers*
	The Houses By The Green
	Miniatures
Rosalyn Drexler	*The Investigation* and *Hot Buttered Roll*
Harrison, Melfi, Howard	*New Short Plays*
Duffy, Harrison, Owens	*New Short Plays: 2*
Henry Livings	*Good Grief!*
	The Little Mrs Foster Show
	Honour and Offer
	Pongo Plays 1–6
John McGrath	*Events While Guarding the Bofors Gun*
David Mercer	*The Governor's Lady*
Georges Michel	*The Sunday Walk*
Rodney Milgate	*A Refined Look At Existence*
Guillaume Oyono-Mbia	*Three Suitors: One Husband* and *Until Further Notice*
Alan Plater	*Close the Coalhouse Door*
David Selbourne	*The Play of William Cooper and Edmund Dew-Nevett*
	The Two-Backed Beast
	Dorabella
Johnny Speight	*If There Weren't Any Blacks You'd Have to Invent Them*
Martin Sperr	*Tales From Landshut*
Boris Vian	*The Knacker's ABC*
Lanford Wilson	*Home Free!* and *The Madness of Lady Bright*